MILTON GLASER

PREFACE BY JEAN MICHEL FOLON

MILTON GLASER   GRAPHIC DESIGN

THE OVERLOOK PRESS, WOODSTOCK, NEW YORK

This book was printed by the
Dai Nippon Co., Ltd., Tokyo;
Text matter was set in 8pt. Helvetica Light
by Metro Typographers Inc., New York.
Display type is Neo–Futura, designed by
Milton Glaser and provided by
Photolettering, Inc., New York.
For a hardcover edition of this work,
spine bound in cloth, write to
The Overlook Press, Woodstock, New York, 12498

Enpapers are details of poster on page 205

DEDICATION
For Rudi

ACKNOWLEDGMENTS
My deepest thanks to
George Leavitt for his friend-
ship and invaluable help in
producing this book; also to
Hildy Maze for her good
spirits, hard work, and bad
spelling. To Claudine Vernier
for her photographs and
translations from the French;
to Peter Mayer for his
planning, patience, and
relentless pursuit of
excellence.

PREFACE

The first time I met Milton we had an appointment in the jungle. To get there I took the *metro* to the center of Paris, then a bus to the airport. After a plane ride, I arrived in the jungle and rented a canoe. Paddling down river, all the beauty of the world was displayed before me, as though the world were an enormous drawing by Milton Glaser, moving with the wind. Long green plants were bent with the weight of birds. One thing seemed strange to me: Where was that dazzling light surrounding everything coming from? I left the boat on the river bank. Milton could have arranged to meet me at the Café de Flore in Saint-Germain des Prés, but no, it had to be the jungle. A bit tired, I sat down on a large comfortable rock and waited patiently there in the jungle. A strange world came alive; red, green, and blue trees seemed to be flat tints of color. High up on a branch Bob Dylan was singing. His skin was black, his hair a rainbow. All this would have pleased Milton, but where was he? Suddenly, a large hand placed itself near me. It seemed to invite me. It was then that I raised my eyes. In the dazzling light I saw a gigantic figure, a strange being. He was wearing round glasses. It was Milton himself. And for hours I had been sitting on his shoe! Climb on my hand, said he. And his hand rose like an elevator. Reaching eye level, face-to-face, I didn't quite know what to say to him. He didn't speak either. From this height we dominated the forest. We were mute before so much beauty. A little further away someone gave me a friendly wave. I recognized one of Milton's colleagues. Looking around, on branches in the trees, other artists, friends of Milton, drawing. So that's The Studio; I never imagined it this way, I told Milton. He said nothing and started to draw. On the paper a sun appeared with bursting rays, the sun we know so well from his pictures. I looked up at the sky for his model, but there was no sun that day. The dazzling light that had intrigued me in the canoe came from the paper itself. And I suddenly understood where the sun came from. It was Milton who brought it with him. Folon

INTRODUCTION

The following text is an edited version of a lengthy conversation taped in September 1972; it was edited in April 1973 with this book in mind, only deleting those questions and answers not directed to the thrust of the present work. Peter Mayer's questions are in blue—Milton Glaser's responses are in black.

Is there a difference between design and art?

Several, but they are not as obvious as one might suspect. In some areas the objectives of art and design are harmonious and congruent. Confusion often arises in those instances when the disciplines and objectives are separate. In design, there is a given body of information that must be conveyed if the audience is to experience the information. That objective is primary in most design activities. On the other hand, the essential function of art is to change or intensify one's perception of reality.

Through most of history perception and information existed simultaneously in works of art. The stained glass windows at Chartres tell the story of the stations of the cross to a nonliterate public . . . and great artists were used to that end. As society developed the information and the art function diverged, and distinctions were made between high art and communicating information to increasing numbers of people. High art, of course, is supposed to have the more elevating characteristics.

When you are asked to help ''sell'' a product, do you see yourself as going beyond the public's consciousness of the product, changing people's perceptions, in other words?

Perhaps the answer can be found by indirection: the reason new forms usually don't emerge from the design activity—as they do in what we'll call the art activity—is that design in many ways is a vernacular language. Design-related work assumes that the audience addressed has an *a priori* understanding of the vocabulary. The essential heart of most art activity is the self-expressive potentiality that the form offers, enlarging therefore the possibilities for the invention of new modes of perception for both the artist and the audience. Meaningful works address us in a way that alters our perception of our reality. Walking past a forest it is possible to say, ''That looks like a Cezanne,'' the implication being that Cezanne has altered our visual perception of forests. Design works differently. It conveys information based on the audience's previous understanding. Because design deals with familiar forms, much of it depends on the cliché. In fact, the study of cliché as a mode of expression is fundamental to an understanding of design. Clichés are symbols or devices that have lost their power and magic; yet they persist because of some kind of essential truth. Clichés are fundamental sources of information, debased sources waiting to receive new energy. In design, as in so many other things—from human relationships to logotypes—frequent contact often produces immunity to the experience. Two things can help here; an attempt to maintain an innocent vision and the capacity to respond to internal and external changes.

Do you feel that there is a moral aspect to your work, or perhaps to graphic design in general?

I think that attempts to deal with the relationship between art and morality are very complex.

Perhaps I'm alluding to a designer's responsibility to the society, if he has one.

One can see the complexity in the difficulties some designers who work for ad agencies are experiencing now. The sense is growing that much work produced by advertising agencies may be harmful to the community addressed.

Does that concern you?

Intensely. But I feel that anyone involved in communications comes up against that problem . . . and always has. Now we're beginning to realize that all aspects of communication, whatever the form, have extraordinary implications to the community receiving the information. And so we can't afford not to pay attention to the quality of information that is distributed. In fact, we know that a comic strip may have a more profound effect on its community than a work of Picasso. For that reason alone, a critical examination of banal graphic phenomena is a worthy investigation indeed. Recent critical attention paid to comic strips and posters support that idea. In other words, it's important to have a critical view of these artifacts because they are so terribly significant in establishing the mythology and the ethos of a people.

Because one can clearly see in your work a continuing interest in the historical sources of the communication of ideas, as well as the persistence of forms, I wonder if there was something in your student years at Cooper Union, or later in Italy, that led to your interest in style and tradition.

At Cooper Union, like most students, I studied the fundamentals and was fortunately exposed to a world of many stylistic alternatives. At Bologna, studying with Giorgio Morandi, I encountered a classical past and met a great man.

Why do you work in so many styles?

15

Psychically I know it has a lot to do with boredom, with my inability to sustain interest in one form or to be committed to one form of expression for any length of time. At one point in my life I realized that anything I did long enough to master was no longer useful to me. I've always felt that I could explore many phenomena, that, in fact, the whole visual history of the world was my resource. But I really can't say how my interest in many styles developed. Perhaps out of weakness. Perhaps there was an incapacity to deal with certain kinds of problems or to solve them in one idiom. You could say that self-expressive activities have their source as much in a person's inability to deal with certain kinds of problems as in anything else. So I can't really say why my own interest has always been in essentially breaking down the expectation of what design should be. One of the things I decided early on was that as a designer I didn't have to be committed to either design, typography, or illustration, that I could, in fact, design a store or make a toy. When I entered the field there was a very rigid distinction between the designer and the illustrator, in terms of function. There were very few designers who illustrated and very few illustrators who had any idea of how to design. My desire to exercise as much control over my own work as I could usually kept me away from situations in which I would have to entrust my illustration to someone else's notion of design. George Salter, a teacher of mine at Cooper Union, was a major influence. He was an excellent calligrapher and also an illustrator. I feel that his work always had that unity and conviction that emerges from dealing with the total surface. But you can only exercise that broad control if your understanding of technique, culture, and history are broad. Obviously everything that you've ever seen in your life has the potential to be integrated into your work, but it's hard to take advantage of that fact.

I've often heard people say, "Well, that looks like Milton Glaser's work." Aren't those people responding, in many cases, to one aspect of your work that has become broadly imitated? How do you feel about imitation?

Well, I don't feel personally limited by third party elements. After all, no artist is really trivialized by what others do with his work. It's certainly not my concern. Imitation is interesting, although there's a distinction between influence and imitation. Distortions occur in the surface qualities of imitated work. These are heightened and become the pervasive element of the work. Imitation has a cultural function, after all. It aids in defining and popularizing a style. The school of Rubens defines and illuminates Rubens. We all begin by imitation. The penalty for consistent imitation, unfortunately, is the erosion of personal vision and artistic sensibility. My central concern, however, is not with others. I'm trying to use design activity as a device for personal growth. On the best level one's activity as a designer can be an extraordinary mechanism for self-realization.

In other words, you look for new energy to emerge from your work and have it enrich your whole life?

Right. It's peculiarly appropriate in that sense. Any man's work has the potentiality of being used for that purpose. But there are some peculiar aspects to design activity as it relates to the subject: First of all, one is involved in feedback, the response to information, in a sense, the justification one gets from the work itself. This has nothing to do with the approval that one gets from an audience. Partially it may have to do with producing a physical record that exists in time. The artist and designer have the opportunity to see their work over a ten-year period and seeing the visual or tangible manifestation of certain states of mind it represented. We're talking about a lifetime feedback. Most people don't have access to that kind of information because most jobs don't provide an objective documentation.

Do you ever have a sense in reviewing your work of an emerging sensibility not yet created? A sense of where you're going, in other words?

One can see the roots of certain phenomena in a work before they occur. I mean, you can see a certain kind of move towards a certain kind of form, a certain concern for line or color, whatever it is, beginning to develop. I think part of the reality of the situation is the blindness of the direction. There are always numerous possibilities for solution; you can always justify a choice on the basis of the existing conditions but that doesn't exclude other solutions; it simply means that out of the choices you have at any given moment, for reasons deeply rooted in your psychic life you make a choice, some choice, hopefully the right choice, whatever "right" means.

In a supermarket of choices, how do you begin to solve a design problem?

Basically two possibilities exist. One is the professional response to a given problem that emerges from recognizing previous successful solutions to similar problems. To a large extent using successful formulas with relatively predictable results is professional yet, by definition, noncreative. A more meaningful kind of procedure occurs when the problem is not susceptible to a reliance on previously successful formulas or to an intellectualizing of the content. The creative process is essentially a blind process where you do not prestructure and you have to allow information to arise in a spontaneous way uncontrollable by the will. The best work I've done occurred in that way. The most meaningful developments in my work are those that occurred involuntarily and blindly, without my knowing what I was going to do, when I had enough faith in my own creative process to

be willing to wait for it to happen without my will demanding it.

But in a society where design is demanded by people perhaps not terribly sensitive to design or the problems of the designer, don't you feel the designer is permitting himself the luxury of a waiting period?

I can only say that the best part of my work is that work where that condition existed and the other part of my work which is visible is professionalism.

Can you conceive of another society or work or nation in which the artist would be freer and consequently more creative?

No. I think there's too much ambiguity about the idea of freedom.

You mean we use the word too loosely?

Well, certainly quality in art seems to come as much from restriction as it does from freedom.

When you say "restriction," do you mean external demands?

Right. I mean the history of art demonstrates that great art was produced within a context of severe restriction and specific demands. Much more important than abstract ideas of freedom and restriction relative to art is the qualitative nature of the audience being addressed. The decline of great cooking in Paris can be traced to a subtle re-orientation of the chefs from a cuisine based on informed local patrons to a cuisine prepared for tourists unfamiliar with the tradition. Their ability to pay entitled them to make demands on the chefs but they didn't know what demands to make.

I remember spending a week with you in which we drove through the northern part of Italy chasing down every Piero della Francesca we could find. Was there something in Piero that speaks to some of the things that we're talking about here—whether a relationship with a tradition, or something else—or was it just that we happened to be there? Is there something special that excites you in Piero?

Yes. I feel great personal identification with Piero. Like everyone who has discovered him, I've always felt he was a mysterious artist out of his time. There's no one like him; he's unique. My first strong sympathy for him was at the time I first encountered him; I couldn't believe what I'd discovered; I pursued him all over Italy and I wanted to share that experience with anyone whom I felt deeply about. Of the many aspects of his work that fascinate me, I've always been specially interested in his absolute geometric clarity, the precision, the sense of inevitability. . . .

What do you mean by the sense of inevitability?

Well, the forms in Piero, the composition and the structure, the sense of classicism. We are confronting a sublime intelligence. . . . Nothing in Piero can be altered or changed. It's inevitable, as though nature gave it to us. It's this passionate, cool, precise, geometric ordering of elements in their most perfect relationship that, as a designer, I find beautifully intriguing. At the same time I've always been fascinated by the opposite: the qualities of arbitrary expressionistic disorder. My personal feeling for Piero lies in his perfect realization of half of my interests. I've always been enormously attracted to the polarities, and Piero represents, like Vermeer, a real half, a basic but very significant half that I can experience in the deepest way.

It seems to me that both your frames of reference and your resources encompass broad areas of both American and European life. But, superficially at least, that doesn't seem prescribed by your background.

First of all, I've lived and worked in New York most of my life and New York occupies a peculiar position relative to the rest of America stretching West, and Europe to the East. My own immediate background is European, both my parents coming from Hungary. Like New York itself, I've been nourished by two main cultural experiences. New York is the communication and information center of the world, and the range evident in my work is surely, at least partially, a result of where I work. Also, perhaps being Jewish is a factor too—to the extent that a detachment from a narrow nationalistic identification permits a greater openness to a greater variety of American and European inputs.

What I'm trying to ask about is the range between. . . . Let's talk about specific works . . . your bookcover illustration for Mauriac's *Thérèse,* for example, which seems wholly within the European experience and, let us say, your Dylan poster, which seems to make a uniquely American statement.

If I talk about the Dylan, you'll see what I mean. Perhaps you'll construe your sense of ''range'' differently. The Dylan emerged from two very different conventions. One is the memory echo I had of a silhouette self-portrait that Marcel Duchamps cut out of paper. I remember it very clearly, a simple black and white profile. The convention of Dylan's hair really emerged from certain forms that intrigued me in Islamic painting. The union of those two very disparate stylistic phenomena produced something that you called ''uniquely American,'' right? So it's funny . . . What we're talking about here is believability. What is believable is related to a cultural moment.

To what extent, or at what point, does the cultural moment interact with your aesthetic sensibility and the client's mundane or practical informational needs?

That's hard for me to answer in a clear fashion. I know that it's becoming more difficult for me to work with clients who have a too-clear idea of the aesthetic solution. Frequently clients want performance based on previous solutions; my own tendency is to become less receptive to repeating what I've already done. The situation I find most comfortable now is a situation in which people essentially simply trust that my understanding of the problem is equal to the task.

Would you like the person giving you this assignment to describe the problem, if not the situation, or, minimally, the market he's trying to reach? What do you feel is the freest situation for you consonant with, obviously, the client's need?

I certainly don't rule out a full discussion of the problem. But I go back to the ambiguities I suggested earlier re freedom and restriction. Remember, the freest situation is not necessarily the absence of demand; but if the work is outlined too specifically in its objectives and too precisely in what it hopes to achieve in terms of style, then obviously the work is less useful for me as a growth possibility. And my personal growth is a factor in the conception and execution of the task.

Can you describe a situation in which for one reason or another the client's art director feels you haven't solved his problem? Do you feel you can turn your head around from your first solution—which you believe in—and simply do another?

Yes, if not in every case. There are times when a rejection becomes a limitation to transcend, but the possibility for excellence must always exist as the objective. If the goal, however, is to water down the solution, I find this difficult to respond to. Finally, such requirements, expressed or implicit, become destructive for everybody involved.

How do you feel today about what faces young students in graphics, either relative to their art in a pure sense or relative to the society in which they're going to work?

We spoke earlier of an increasing resistance to advertising as a profession; concurrently there is an increasing willingness of many people in communication to accept the responsibility of doing what they feel is ethically right. They do not want to be destructive to the community for whom they, in theory, work. They put themselves midway between the client and the public, as opposed to being simply an extension of the client. Today absence of urgency is inextricably linked to an unprecedented opportunity for influence through growing communication technology. The same is true for the designer involved in creating products for consumption relative to an increasing industrial capacity to produce things. Because we've become increasingly aware that people, resources, and institutions are inter-related in a global, and perhaps even cosmic way, those involved in communicating myths, morals, news, and ideologies, have a central position and a unique responsibility.

Are you really discussing a design revolution relative to solutions for the problems of our society?

Well, I think that may be phrased too portentously. The issue may be more a question of self-realization than revolution.

Since we have spoken about shifting societal patterns, how do you feel about individual achievement as it relates to group efforts?

One's individual contribution and perception is most useful when it's shared. One of the things that is emerging is the capability of everyone to view his own life as an artistic entity. We're perceiving more and more that the separation between artist and non-artist is becoming much more difficult to maintain. Every life has a potential creative or artistic content. At this time we recognize the possibility of integrating art and life. This will result in considerable discomfort to those people whose status comes out of being creative in a hierarchical sense. The possibility for seeing the relationship between art and life can be perceived in the design experience, although not exclusively. There is something in the act of composition, of moving things around until one finds a tough and expressive way for them to relate to each other that is also applicable in a temporal sense to one's living experience.

Undoubtedly, there are limits to what one can maintain for the design experience, but I believe that it is unique in that so much of our perception is visual. Neurologically, 80% of what we experience we experience through our eyes, so that many of the basic assumptions we make about the nature of life is visual. Many of our limitations also come out of that perception, the fact that we don't really use our other senses in an even proximate relationship to their potential. The visual experience is obviously the one with the greatest conditioning effect on us and those of us who work in the visual field can translate that phenomenon perhaps most easily into our lives.

Do the new media and technology, in your opinion, have an important effect on the designer and his work?

Let me make a generality about how a designer or an artist works at his best level. The best work emerges from the observation of phenomena that exist independently of each other. What the designer intuits is the linkage, singular or plural. He sees a way to unify separate occurrences and create a gestalt, an experience in which this new unity provides a new insight. It doesn't really matter, in a sense, what the subject matter is . . . or the means to convey it . . . What is essential is the perception of the linkages between phenomena. So whatever it is, whether it's time and space or heat or light or you and me . . . the critical act is to understand the linkages and to bring phenomena that have never been unified into some kind of unity. That's what design is about and that's what art is about, and it doesn't really matter what the media considerations are.

FROM POPPY WITH LOVE

The problem concerned a
request for a poster to intro-
duce and promote a new
record company which saw
itself as breaking with con-
ventional practices. The image
of a bright flower breaking
through a stone monolith
reflects the client's view of
his relationship to the
industry. Ironically, after a
certain degree of success,
Poppy Records was sold to
one of the established
monoliths.

1

(2)
This poster announced a show of Art Deco design, artifacts, and furniture. I used the checkerboard and ziggurat forms in combination with a modified chevron because they had obvious associations with the movement. The overlapping letterforms are also characteristic of the period. I took liberties with color. An interesting job technically: It only ran through the press twice, using the Split Fount technique, employing a variety of inks on each roller of the press. In printing, these colors blend and a multi-color effect results more common in silk screen than in offset reproduction. It was printed on pale yellow paper, once again intensifying the total color effect.

20

AMERICA'S GRAPHIC DESIGN MAGAZINE
JANUARY/FEBRUARY 1971
PRINT XXV:I

Print

(3)
I was asked to do an Art Deco cover for *Print,* a graphic arts magazine. I used the facing page poster (2), as raw material and "cannibalized" it. I reassembled the pieces as a three-dimensional construction lighted from below and photographed it, achieving a different effect from the same elements.

21

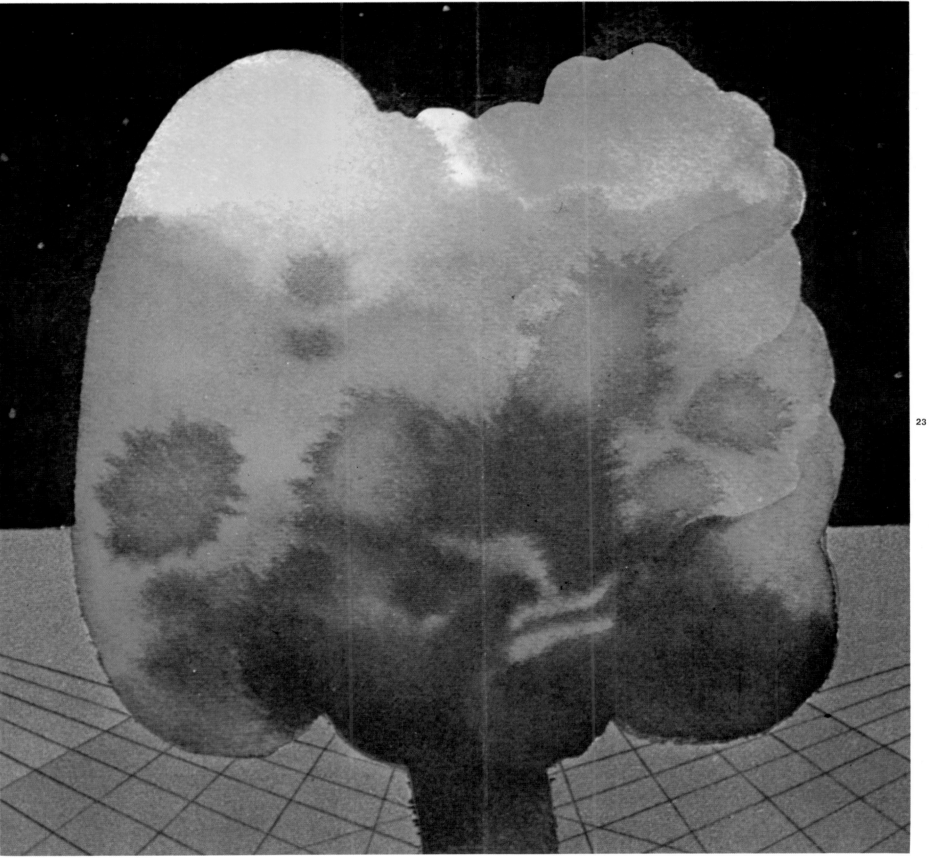

24

6

On the previous page (4, 5), two details from the Bach poster (6) It's obviously not easy to graphically encompass the range of Bach's work. Personal associations for me—particularly in terms the music's structure and geometry—were details from an Islamic rug, a series of geometric references including grids, overlapping discs, and a variety of perspective lines. References to certain natural forms—leaves, trees, landscapes—point to pastoral aspects in Bach's work. Surfaces are somewhat more fragmented than is usually considered desirable, particularly for posters. The form of the tree and that of Bach's head and collar are identical. Perhaps this particular graphic trick has been expressed too subtly; most people miss the overlapping images. But it's nice to leave something for later. Bach's signature was a particularly attractive graphic element.

(7)
This poster was done about a year later. There are obvious references to the Bach poster (6), particularly in the idea of the central tree with a landscape underscoring a one-point perspective. The background is a ''dead steal'' from one of Piero della Francesca's landscapes.

7

We Wish You a Merry Christmas, We Wish You a Merry Christmas, We Wish You a Merry Christmas, and a Happy New Year!

A New Year's greeting for a company making films. The firm's two partners were after a dramatic Christmas greeting which led to considerable discussion as to who was carrying whom. Again the Split Fount technique, achieving maximal color with two plates. In much of my work, including the examples (6, 7), I employ the accidental effects characteristic of ink and water colors blending when wet. In the case of Split Fount, the original work must be done in black and white. All color adjustments occur on the press; the first time one sees the precise color relationships. Unfortunately, few printers have the time, interest, or talent for it.

(9)
This poster was conceived as a fold-out bonus for *Eye,* a magazine that sought to combine youth, hipness, and establishment advertising. The forms make reference to both Art Deco and Matisse. I am fond of the relationship between the large and small forms and of the way the lettering echoes the portrait's decorative sense. I was concerned with expressing power and energy. Working from photographs as source material for portraiture is an ongoing problem for designers and illustrators. The insistence of the original photographic source often makes itself detrimentally felt in the final work. Another problem is capturing likeness. I'm not highly skilled at it and try to compensate with other kinds of graphic input.

26

9

Originally intended as a poster for a new Joan Baez record, the whole project was killed midstream. I never completed the portrait but in retrospect I think it is more successful unfinished than it would have been completed.

27

10

(11)
My wife Shirley served as the
model for this book jacket.
This is the work that Peter
Mayer refers to as being
"wholly within the European
experience" in the intro-
duction.

11

This drawing was part of a series in which each work was executed by a different member of the Push Pin Studio, each working with identical elements. A small portrait of Ché is in the bottom right of each illustration, the drawing recapitulating the same elements.

This work deals with the notion of wholeness and fragmentation, reality and myth. I still find the original photograph extremely touching and powerful. The illustration was done for *Ramparts*, a magazine whose audience identified strongly with Guevara.

29

Here I was trying to demonstrate a fundamental crazi-
ness that seemed to surround
Jack Ruby in the Kennedy-
Oswald-Ruby developments.
The letter accompanying the
illustration in *Ramparts* gives
a clear indication of his
basic insanity. I used
many portraits of Ruby done
in a variety of styles to echo
the situation's complexity
and ambiguity. Curiously,
what contributes most to the
feeling of insanity is the
way the figure is set in the
space; the grid serves to
emphasize the diagonal
disruption of the figure.

30

A Letter
from Jail
by
Jack
Ruby

MILTON GLASER

13

(14)
This portrait, one of a series
of "fat men in history," was
done for the *Push Pin
Monthly Graphic,* the studio's
own magazine, which I
might add, appears irregu-
larly. Various crank diets
were part of the accompanying text. I like the effect of
pencil on a highly textured
paper, in this case Strath-
more. Drawing of this sort is
very effective done small and
blown up for reproduction.
Seurat, of course, did the
definitive drawings in this style.

(15, 16)
These two drawings appear
on facing pages in the
Graphic. The subject of the
issue was "Good and Evil."
We attempted to develop
two separate biographies for
a variety of historical figures,
one demonstrating ostensible
good, the other ostensible
evil. I started with a wash
drawing of the Marquis de
Sade and used photostats to
stretch the drawing. In some
way the idea of elevation
suggested the affirmative
side of one's character. On
the facing page (16), using
the same original, I com-
pressed the image. It's very
easy to get corny when
attempting to represent
abstract ideas, particularly
those involving either moral
principles or deep feelings.
This solution may be somewhat over-intellectualized.

32

Donation Alphonse
Francoise de Sade

Born in 1740
the Marquis de Sade
began his life studying
in the Benedictine
and Jesuit schools and
went on to a successful
military career,
achieving the rank of
cavalry captain at
twenty three, when he
was discharged. As
a people's representative
to the National
Convention in 1790,
he was active in the
revolutionary government
and wrote several
political tracts and
pamphlets. His Dialogue
between a Priest and
a Dying Man, written in
1782, was an astonishingly
enlightened attack on the
deity and clerical
establishment. The "Fifth
Dialogue" of Philosophy in
the Bedroom, known as
"Yet Another Effort,
Frenchmen, If You Would
Become Republicans"
clearly establishes
de Sade's opposition to
and abhorrence of fascism.

15

**Donation Alphonse
Francoise de Sade**

On October 29, 1763, five
months after his marriage,
de Sade is sent to prison for
the first time. He is charged
with committing excesses
in a brothel which he
frequented. He is released
in a few months but
continues to be involved
in various scandals and
incidents with other women.
In 1768 he is accused of
flogging and, in general,
abusing a young pastry
cook's assistant and again
goes to prison briefly.
In 1772 he is found guilty
of poisoning and sodomy
and sentenced to death. He
escapes and in June of 1778
a High Court nullifies the
sentence on insufficient
evidence but orders new
investigations of allegations
of pederasty and
libertinage. De Sade's
imprisonments and
releases continued until
1801 when he was
finally incarcerated for
the rest of his life.
He died in 1814 at
Chareton Prison.

(17)
Over a period of years I discovered that my best portraits were of men with beards. I've done lots of them. This one is Walt Whitman. The recent increase in mustaches and other facial hair has been a boon to my work.

34

17

The inspiration for the self-portrait was a view of myself glimpsed in the window next to my drawing board at night. It was dark and I could only see the highlight of my nose and glasses. I enjoy drawings in which little information is given and the viewer must imagine the details. The original was done in brown and black crayon, highlighted with white crayon. Working with crayon forces me away from my natural linear inclinations.

(19)
Look asked me for a portrait of Socrates to illustrate a series of articles on the ideas of great men. I was given a list of subjects which the editors felt represented his influence. Using the words as background, I imposed the silhouette over them. The circular forms have a tenuous relationship to Socrates' philosophical and aesthetic system.

36

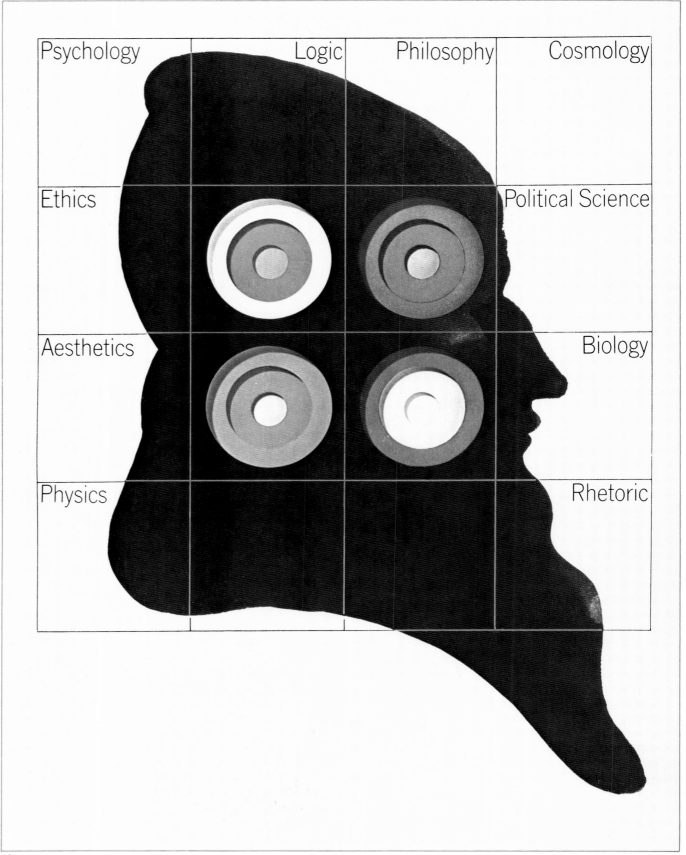

Psychology Logic Philosophy Cosmology

Ethics Political Science

Aesthetics Biology

Physics Rhetoric

This portrait was used on the jacket of a book written by W.C. Fields' companion. She saw herself as his pillar and support and the illustration expresses that idea, particularly since Fields emerges as an extremely infantile personality in the book.

37

HERMANN HESSE

Rosshalde

22

HERMANN HESSE

If the War Goes On…

23

HERMANN HESSE

Autobiographical Writings

24

HERMANN HESSE

Narcissus and Goldmund

NOONDAY 343 $2.25

25

(21-25)
The design goal of individual works in a series is to impart a sense of both continuity and variation. A clear serial relationship must initially be established. In the case of these books, I used a strong typographical style and a close-cropped portrait of Hesse on each cover. The variation is achieved by changing the style and color of each. The portraits roughly relate to the period of each book's publication. I was particularly fortunate because Hesse went through some dramatic physical changes from his youth to his old age. The portrait (21), appeals to me, perhaps because, again, it gives the least information. Someone once asked if I was thinking about the Hessian idea of many lives in one body when I did these covers. I told him it was a fortunate coincidence.

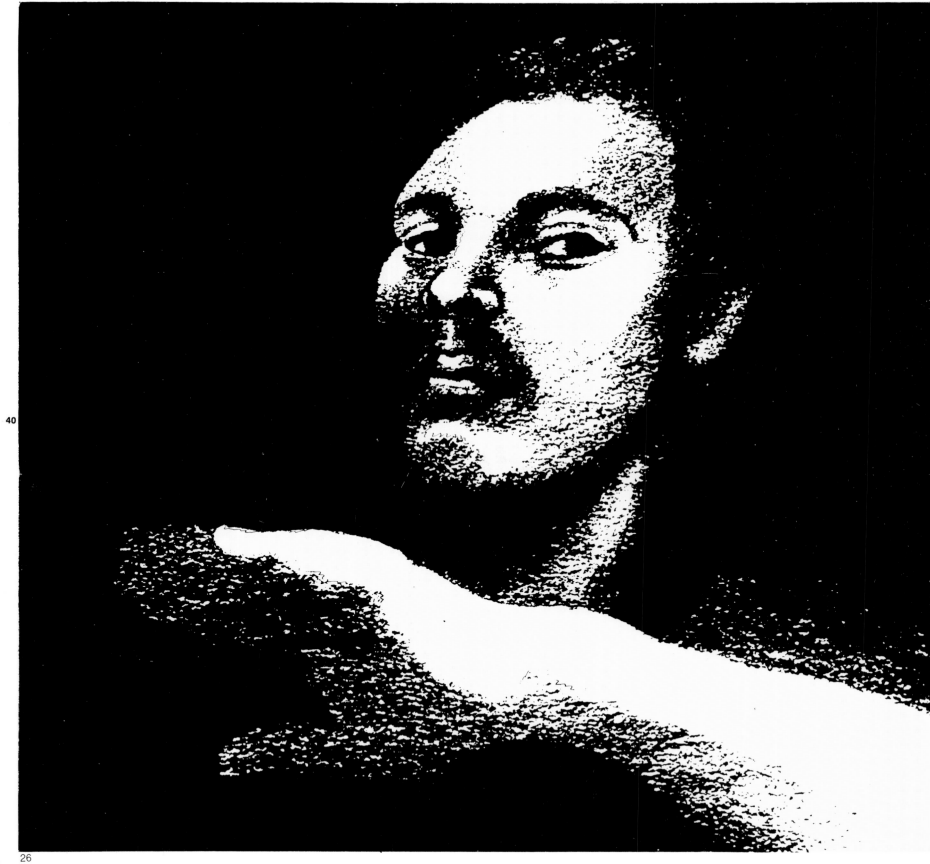

These drawings for *New York*, a magazine whose graphics I helped develop, illustrate an article by Oscar Lewis on Puerto Rican life in the city. The drawings are imaginary portraits. I wanted the drawings strong in texture, matching the strength and liveliness of Lewis's piece. They were enlarged from small pencil drawings.

27

28

29

30

31

(28-31)
The four heads on the left
were done for a printing firm
to demonstrate a variety of
their printing techniques. All
are details of larger drawings.

(32)
This drawing was used as
the cover for another Hesse
work, *Steppenwolf*, unrelated
by design to the previous
series and actually created
six or eight years earlier.

(33)
Ideas for this jacket emerged directly from the fact that the poet's name always appeared in lower-case. Whenever a design solution emerges from given peculiarities, there's a sense of inevitability about the solution. If the observation is too obvious, we feel the artist is taking a "cheap shot." In cases where the relationship between question and answer is more penetrating, the results can be very satisfying. The author of this book hated the jacket.

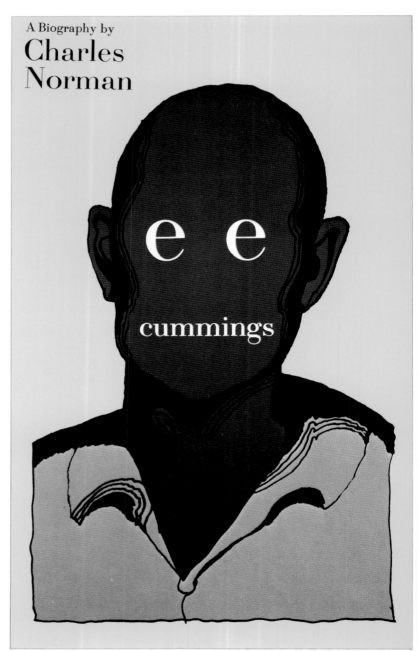

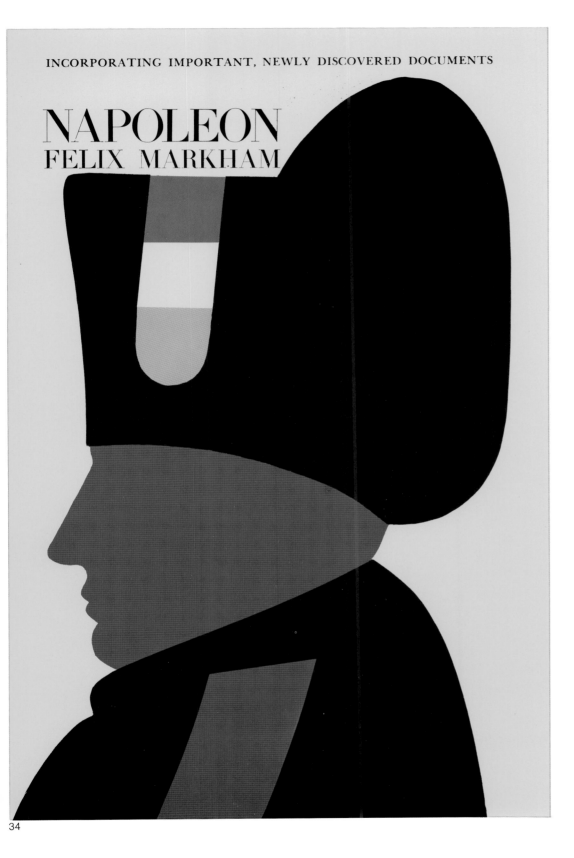

INCORPORATING IMPORTANT, NEWLY DISCOVERED DOCUMENTS

NAPOLEON
FELIX MARKHAM

Obviously the profile of Napoleon is not drawn here with any great sense of likeness; fortunately, the shape of his hat is so identifiable as to guarantee recognition.

(35)
In 1961 I approached *Esquire* with an idea for a spread in their Christmas issue showing the diversity of style in representations of the head of Christ. I was interested in the range of variation possible in depicting a single limited subject. Every example was found within a few days from easily available sources in New York. Of course, they represent only a fraction of the possible examples. The second head down in the left-hand column is supposed to be a Haitian primitive. It was actually drawn by my wife, Shirley. All the others are "authentic."

35

(36)
There are certain themes and images that seem to recur in my work, such as the skull. Gathering materials for this book, I became aware of how often I used this image. Here the illustration was for an article in *Vista,* a United Nations magazine, on the economics of the international drug trade.

WELCOME TO THE CLUB
a novel by Clement Biddle Wood

How much information to convey to a potential reader on a dust jacket is a crucial question for the designer. The problem is not so much representing the contents of the book, but rather not mis-representing them. This particular work conveys relatively little information, but it does stop the reader long enough to engage his interest. I've always been unhappy about the relationship between the two kinds of type at the top. For the second line I chose type somewhat lighter in weight, but the publisher was apprehensive about its read-ability. A heavier face was substituted. The tensions between the artist's objec-tives and his client's needs can either enhance or weaken a solution. The final result depends on the intelli-gence, talent, and person-alities of the people involved.

(38, 39)
This silhouette cutout by
Marcel Duchamps (38), was
in the back of my mind when
I created the Dylan poster
(39). This particular piece is
probably the most familiar of
my works, if only for the fact
that nearly six million were
produced for enclosure in a
Dylan album. One day a
French photographer visited
the Studio and told the following story: He was on
assignment traveling up the
Amazon and stopped in a
village of about one hundred
Indians. He entered a hut
and, as his eyes grew accustomed to the darkness, he
saw the Dylan poster on the
wall. He never was able to
find out how it got there. In
addition to the Duchamps
silhouette, the other significant graphic element in this
piece is the quality, shape,
and color of the hair. In some
ways these elements were
influenced by my interest in
Islamic painting. As I mentioned earlier in the introduction, the combination of the
Duchamps portrait and Near
Eastern design elements
produced a style some now
consider peculiarly American.

50

38

40

41

G. Keys Presents

MAHALIA JACKSON
EASTER SUNDAY
PHILHARMONIC HALL
LINCOLN CENTER

Sunday, March 26, 1967 4:00 & 8:30 P.M.
TICKETS: 5.50, 5.00, 4.50, 4.00,
3.50, 2.95 Tickets Available at:
Lincoln Center Box Office &
Bloomingdales TR 4-2424

42

(40-43)
This poster of Mahalia Jackson was printed in two parts, one facing left (41), the other facing right (42). It was designed to produce different effects in different arrangements according to the available display space.

43

(44)
I developed this image of a G-cleŕ growing into a blossom for the first Ambler Music Festival at Temple University. It has continued to serve as a symbol for the festival since then.

Ambler Music Festival / Institute of Temple University

Temple University Music Festival and Institute

This poster was done one year later, an attempt to continue the idiom of the music staff and flowers. It is quite decorative but doesn't seem to have the impact or the memorable qualities of the original. You win some, you lose some. Since then the Festival has returned to the original, adding another flower each year to the clef.

(46)
Commissioned by the Russian Tea Room, a New York restaurant, this poster celebrated a series of jazz concerts. The gesture of the Russian pouring vodka into a saxophone may not be expressed clearly enough in terms of visual impact.

46

This poster announced an exhibition of toys designed by artists. The representation of the artist as a toy really doesn't work if you pursue the logic of that image. Fortunately, the words clearly express the content of the show. Spirit wins out over logic.

(48, 49)
The drawing on yellow paper
(48) was my original sketch
for a Museum of Modern Art
poster for a show on Dada
and Surrealism. The most
significant difference from
sketch to finish (49) took
place when I moved the word
''Surrealism'' under the table.
I'm very fond of this particular piece, although the
museum wasn't; they re-
jected it.

48

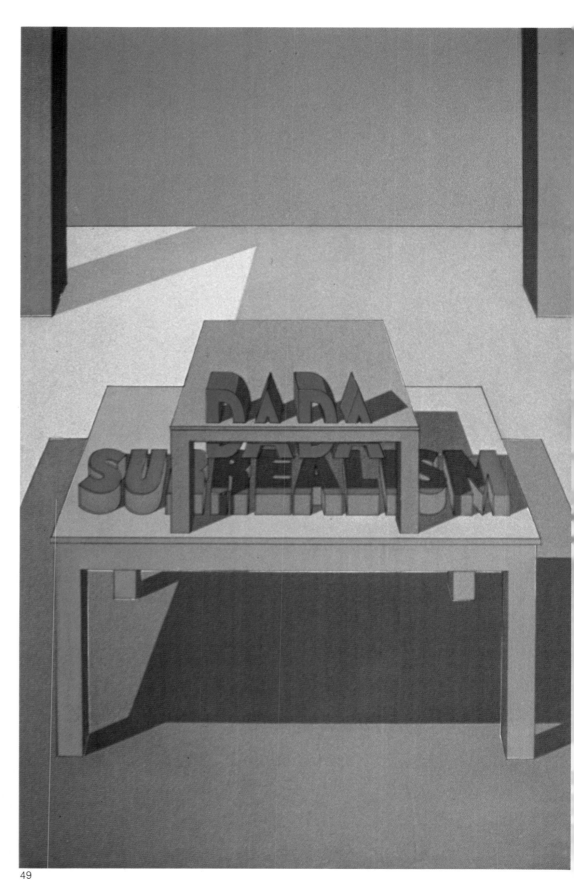

49

(50)
Surrealism has been an enormous influence on my work as it has been on much of American illustration. This drawing done for *Show* when Henry Wolf was the magazine's art director is indebted to Max Ernst and the collages he constructed from old engravings in the Thirties. It also demonstrates my continued interest in cross-hatching as a technique. Much of this emerged from Morandi's influence, particularly in the field of etching.

(51, 52)
A more recent example of
cross-hatching, drawn for an
album, Mozart's *Don Gio-
vanni*. In looking at this piece,
I'm struck by how much of
my work uses comic book
shapes and references. Here
they are enriched by allu-
sions to traditional engraving
and etching techniques. Usually when cross-hatching, I
work horizontally or vertically
or at a forty-five degree diagonal. This procedure can
lead to mechanical results if
one in not careful.

51

(53)
This drawing for the Christmas issue of the *Graphic*
was a transitional one for me.
Until then I had only rarely
expressed the point at which
a form goes from light to
shadow with an enclosing
line. It's particularly clear in
the area around the eyes
and the nose bridge. The
cross-hatching here is quite
loose and open. The style of
my signature also dates this
drawing. In recent years my
signature has become much
more flamboyant and considerably more difficult to read.

(54)
This drawing was based on
an early Italian mannerist
painting. The performer on
this record album felt a particular affinity for the theme
and requested its use for the
cover. The cross-hatching
itself is much more con-
trolled than in the example
on the left. I particularly like
what happens when the
curved lines intersect. Something about the controlled
quality of this drawing makes
the effect quite non-erotic,
although this wasn't my
intention.

62

53

LEDA   LINDA COHEN

(55)
The detail from a painting by Piero de Cosimo served as the inspiration for a poster advertising a new Olivetti typewriter. The original in the National Gallery in London shows a dog mourning over the body of his slain master. I cropped it, added the typewriter to the landscape, and changed the technique from painting to a colored drawing. Actually, the cropping intensifies the original's surreal quality. I'm convinced that Olivetti is the only company in the world that would have accepted a poster of this kind to advertise a typewriter. One of the things I've discovered through the years is that I work best for clients I like. Recently it has become almost impossible for me to work for anyone I don't like: a highly unprofessional attitude. The cross-hatching on the dog's body establishes the weight and solidity of the form. I'm still surprised that the whole thing was ever printed.

I have not included work done through advertising agencies in this book primarily because most advertising assignments are conceived and pre-structured in the agency before an illustrator or designer is commissioned. To keep clients happy, agencies must display superior understanding of the product, while convincing them of the agency's unique creative skills. Before an illustrator is engaged, copy and sketches created by the agency have been seen and approved by the client. What remains is effective execution. Since the opportunity of making a conceptual contribution is absent, I find most advertising work less than fully satisfying.

(56)
This study sought to establish a theme for a motion picture based on the Altamont rock festival at which a murder occurred. It was rejected. I've had very poor luck working for people in the movie business; usually too many are involved, most of them hopelessly confused about artistic-commercial considerations. There is usually great anxiety surrounding projects in which great sums of money are at stake, and the tendency is to fall back on familiar formulae. Besides, the client just didn't like this drawing.

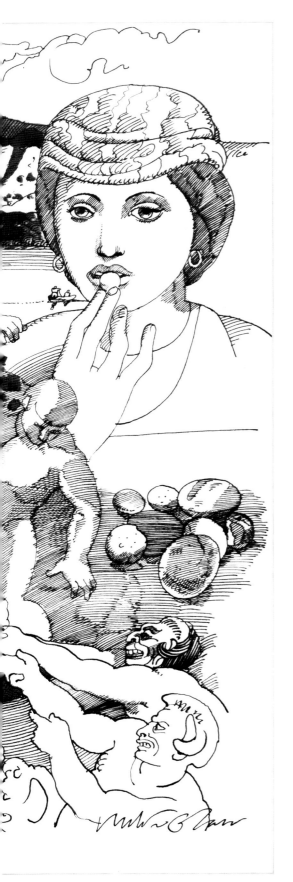

(57-62)
The drawings on the next six pages illustrate an edition of Byron's *Don Juan* annotated by Isaac Asimov. The annotation was quite extensive, exceeding the length of the poem itself. I tried to echo the complexity and richness of the poem and the commentary by executing a series of drawings that had an almost "annotated" quality themselves. I used images that came out of both Byron's and Asimov's writing, arranged in an overlapping, sometimes irrational, juxtaposition. My procedure in these drawings was to read the poem and identify the themes that seemed potentially interesting graphically. I gathered visual reference material from a variety of picture sources including the New York Public Library picture collection (an invaluable source for artists). Usually the sketch took about a day to complete and the finished drawing a day or a day and a half, depending on its complexity and my mood. As technique, I used very little cross-hatching in these drawings, preferring to shade with a variety of parallel lines. Much of this decision was purely professional: I knew that a fully hatched drawing would take three or four times longer. This is not quite as cynical as it sounds at first. A crucial part of being professional in the graphic arts business is understanding what can be achieved in a restricted time framework. I have sometimes been forced to short-change jobs by not spending enough time on them, but I don't feel that is the case here.

60

62

(63)
The drawing inside the eye-
glasses on this dust jacket
for a novel by the Spanish
writer Cela might be over-
looked if it weren't for the fact
that the only color appears
there.

63

(64)
The spiritual erosion of a young man was the essential content of a book for which these drawings were produced as a basis for the jacket. I did the original drawing on the upper left, photostatted it, worked some more on the drawing, then another photostat, continued to work, etc. Finally I had eight photostatted drawings and the original at the lower right, which I colored. The idea is probably too complicated for a paperback cover which should make a simple graphic statement to sell on impulse.

(65, 66)
This drawing illustrated a story in *Audience* (a magazine I will discuss later) about a man whose head was on crooked. Instead of showing him standing straight with a tilted head, I made his head straight and tilted the body. The diagonal of this figure gives the illustration its impact and its surreal perversity. Observe the difference between the original drawing in black and white (65) and the printed work with color added (66). In working for reproduction, the best results can be achieved very often—from the point of view of color and clarity—by drawing the original in black and white. Then a color study is done to guide the engraver who adds the color through photo-mechanical means with a variety of dot screens. The effect is cleaner and brighter than results obtained by reproducing a piece of art work in this style with full color camera separations. The limitation is, of course, that no modulated or even shaded color can be expressed in this way, as you can see from this example. Color is essentially flat and what modulation of color occurs emerges from the cross-hatched black plate.

65

67

(67)
Cross-hatching can be done
quite broadly, as in this
example for a poster advertising a drug product. The
hatching is vigorous in its
textural quality and impact.

(68)
This illustration and the
example on the opposite
page are essentially variations of the same technique,
using a black cross-hatched
drawing to establish the form
of the objects, then using the
color in broad flat areas
below the black. The illustration on this page was for
an article in Signature, the
Diners Club magazine, sug-
gesting how good coffee can
be evaluated. I own the blue
coffee pot and it is a favorite
possession.

(69)
This watercolor was originally used as a poster announcing a series of concerts on various campuses around the country. All the performing artists were under contract to Poppy and formed the nucleus of the record company's talent roster. The copy on the poster read ''The Poppy Foundation,'' which at first sounds like a charitable organization. On second thought it served to identify the Poppy talent community. I thought a foot with a flower growing out of it worked well off the title. Foot, foundation . . . get it?

(70)
Yevtushenko, the Russian poet, wrote a beautiful short story reminiscing on his boyhood as a soccer player. It provoked nostalgia. I tried to capture a mood I recalled from my own youth—of that moment at twilight when the ballgame went on although the light had all but disappeared. I think the horizontal bands of color are a bit too insistent, as I look at this now, but otherwise I've always been pleased with this magazine illustration for the story in *Sports Illustrated*.

70

(71)
Audience offered us many opportunities for illustration. Since we designed it at the Studio and functioned both as art directors and illustrators, we naturally gave ourselves some very choice assignments. This watercolor illustrating a story is a double portrait of Nijinsky and Diagilev. I wanted to show Nijinsky principally through the action of his shadow and a glimpse of his feet. In the back of my mind was a beautiful portrait of the dancer by the Russian artist, Bakst, and I didn't want to compete with it.

(72)
Commissioned by *Ramparts,* this illustration is related to a story about the horrors of abortion. *Ramparts'* ideological position and my own inclinations frequently led to excessively dramatic solutions. Although concerned about this tendency, I can't always resist it. Here the abortionist is seen as a monstrous butcher. Ugh!

The inspiration for this dust jacket of *Spoon River Anthology,* a characteristically American work, came from a collection of photographs by a wonderful German photographer, August Sander.
In fact, I've used Sander's photographs frequently as basic inspirational material. Here I've tightened the figure groupings to make the outside shape of the drawings more powerful.

82

73

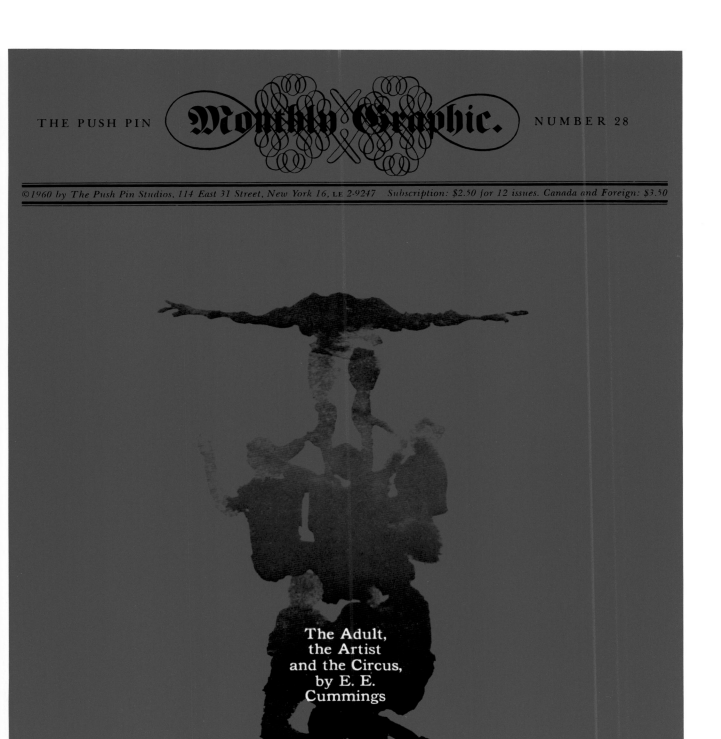

THE PUSH PIN **Monthly Graphic.** NUMBER 28

©1960 by The Push Pin Studios, 114 East 31 Street, New York 16, LE 2-9247   Subscription: $2.50 for 12 issues. Canada and Foreign: $3.50

The Adult,
the Artist
and the Circus,
by E. E.
Cummings

(74)
This cover of the *Graphic* is
an early example of a
technique I've used for more
than fifteen years. I used
blotty, silhouette-like imagery
with very little detail. The
sense of gesture is expressed
primarily by the edges of the
drawing. The influences on
this style came primarily from
Japanese calligraphic wash
drawings and Picasso acqua-
tints. Incidentally, the point
I made earlier about e.e.
cumming's famous use of
lower case seems to have
been lost on me here.

(75)
The cover of another *Graphic* employed the same technique more simply. The danger of nuclear fallout was the subject here.

THE PUSH PIN Monthly Graphic. NO. TWENTY ONE

© 1959 by The Push Pin Studios, 114 East 31 Street, New York 16, LE 2-9247   Subscription $2.50 for 12 issues Canada and Foreign: $3.50

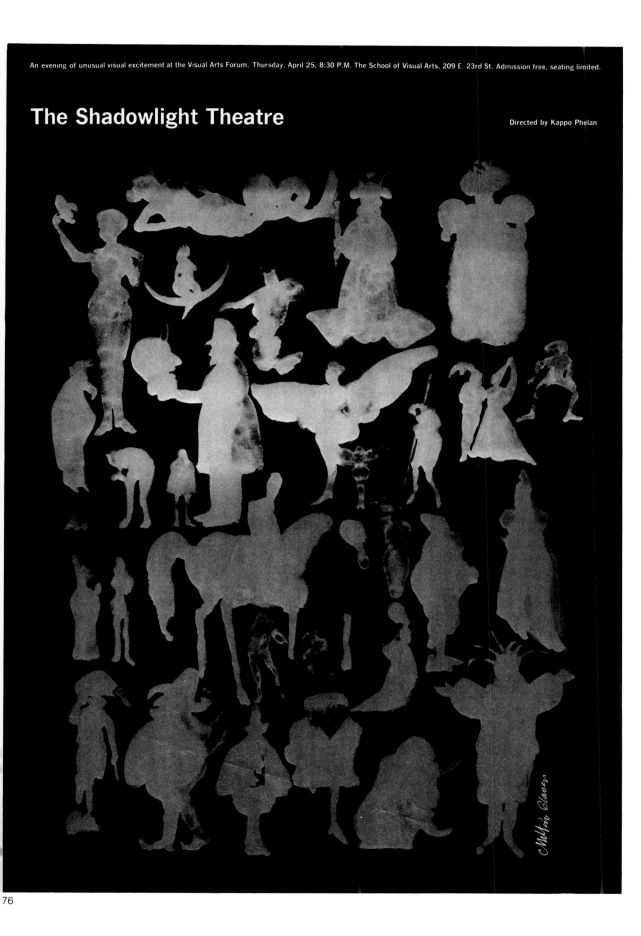

An evening of unusual visual excitement at the Visual Arts Forum, Thursday, April 25, 8:30 P.M. The School of Visual Arts. 209 E. 23rd St. Admission free, seating limited.

The Shadowlight Theatre

Directed by Kappo Phelan

(76)
The Shadowlight Theatre
was a theatrical enterprise
run by a woman named
Kappo Phelan. She created
a modern version of a
Balinese shadow play behind
a screen no larger than a
television set, using cutout
scraps of paper, pieces of
celluloid and glass to produce
tiny theatrical experiences
of unusual visual interest.
I'm always moved by the
combination of humble
materials and intense imagination. What I tried to
capture in this poster was
the sense of light that was a
basic component of this
strange and special theatre.

(77)
More examples of drawings in which the primary concern is gesture, not detail. The effectiveness of such drawings depends on the viewer's willingness to complete the details using his own imagination.

77

(78-81)
More blotchy drawings used as book illustration. Here they work against the precision of typographical forms. The book was a Christmas promotional keepsake commissioned by a typographer. In the original all the devils are red except for the last one; he turns into a green Christmas tree. Its appearance here in blue is a consequence of bookmaking economics. This book was planned for 48 four-color (full color) pages and 192 two-color (black plus one other color) pages. I chose this spread for a two-color section, with blue as a neutral choice.

The Devil's Pi

by ELI CANTOR

Illustrated by Milton Glaser

THE COMPOSING ROOM, INC., NEW YORK

78

In these modern times you might expect all reasonable men to dismiss the attitude of those troubled people with amused tolerance.

But in the dark corners and hell boxes of printshops there are sometimes curious whisperings and rustlings; and many a printer's hair has sometimes stood on end as he suddenly felt himself stared at by unseen eyes, or heard mocking titters rustle softly from the insides of the machines in his plant. Out of those dark corners a strange legend has arisen, hardly ever spoken aloud (whether for fear of ridicule or retribution cannot be said); but sometimes hinted at in guarded tones by old printers when a cup of good cheer has warmed their tongues and made them less careful than usual. It is echoed in the uneasy whispers that pass around a shop when sheets full of errors come from the presses.

Perhaps the legend is only a proofreader's nightmare. Perhaps it has a more solid and horrid basis. Whatever the case may be, we have decided to lift the tale from the shadows of the printshop into the light of day, so that all men may judge for themselves if it be truth or fancy.

If it be true, we shudder to contemplate what revenge the Devil may visit upon us for our boldness in revealing what he has so long kept secret. If, on the other hand, it be fancy,

etaoin shrdlu

aionsh rudl....

8

Satan and his host were bored in hell. After all, eons had passed since their fall from Paradise, and there was a limit to the mischief which even Lucifer's devilish brain could contrive.

Tempting men into sin was no longer a source of amusement. Men yielded too readily.

The imps and demons were restless with pent-up sulphurous energy. Through the mournful gloom of the nether regions they fluttered on nervous wings, like a black horde of locusts. The plains of hell lay forlorn and wild beneath them, half-hidden by the smoke billowing from belching flames sharp with the stench of sulphur.

Satan himself, seated unhappily beside a lake of roaring fire, sighed with ennui. The glimmering of the flames lit up the Archfiend's massive body, and his polished horns seemed spikes of running fire. "Ah," the Devil complained to his faithful captain, Beelzebub, "Hell isn't what it used to be."

"The earth," Beelzebub corrected, "isn't what it used to be. Once men struggled against us, and we enjoyed the thrill of challenge, the delight of battle, the joy of conquering. But now...not only is there no struggle, but Man invents sins that even our ghastly minds would hesitate to conceive. There is nothing left to teach him regarding the horrors of wars, persecutions, oppressions, disasters, perversions and such delights. All foulness Man has made his own and now, indeed, out-devils the Devil himself."

9

79

"To do
aught
good
never
will be
our
task
but
ever to
do ill
our
sole
delight."
Satan

15

𝔄
𝔐erry
𝔊hristmas
and a
𝔥appy
𝔑ew 𝔜ear

MONAURAL—ML 5915

COLUMBIA
MASTERWORKS

Richard Strauss *Don Quixote*
The Philadelphia Orchestra *Eugene Ormandy*
Solo cello: Lorne Munroe *Solo viola: Carlton Cooley*

GUARANTEED
HIGH FIDELITY

© COLUMBIA RECORDS

(82)
In this record cover the Picasso reference is quite obvious. I've always liked the relationship of the script letterforms to the head of Don Quixote.

(83)
The author of this comic horror novel loved the jacket and invited me to dinner at his house. He cooked a frightening meal consisting of a variety of organ meats, most of which I didn't recognize. The book was quite wonderful and was later made into a film with absolutely no relationship to the novel.

a novel

The Cook

Harry Kressing

(84-87)
These drawings of Follies
Girls were done for
an issue of the *Graphic*.
This illustration is an example of an effect that can only
be achieved through the
reproductive process. A
mechanical pattern of dots
such as I used here super-
imposed over the drawing
would be very difficult to
achieve by hand. Printing
technology makes it an
effect easy to achieve. The
investigation of the peculiarities of reproductive
processes can lead the artist
in new directions. At the
same time, I feel that those
who pursue such effects as
their primary interest produce
work which generally is
mediocre. Perhaps in some
recess I have a nagging
moralistic distrust of
technology.

84

94

88

(88-91)
This series of nude drawings
was commissioned for a
book about the human body.

89

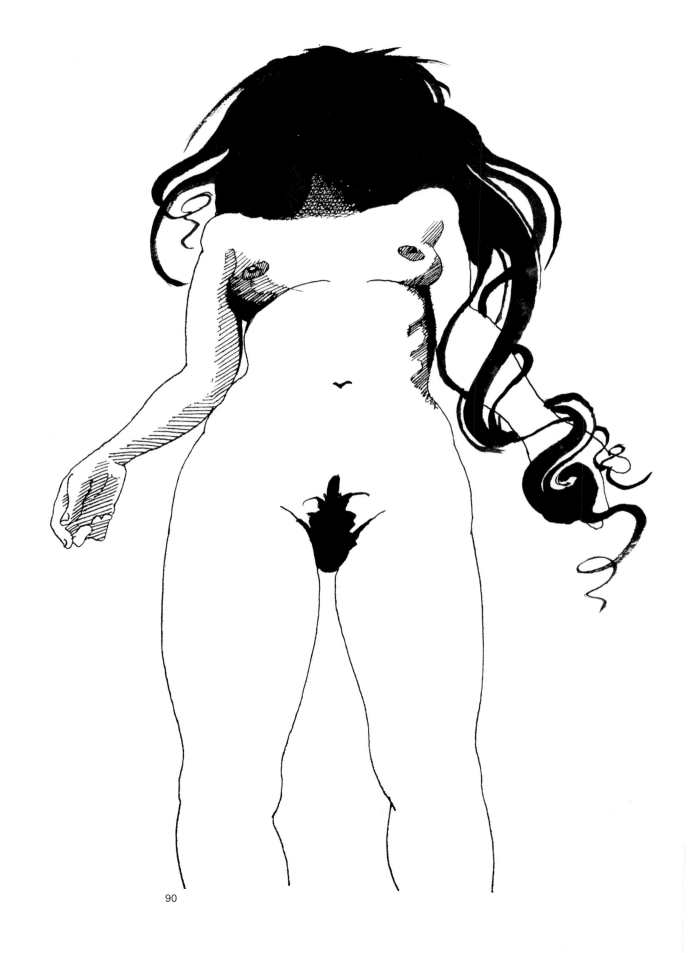

91

(92-94)
The following eight pages come from a *Graphic* on George Méliès, the early French filmmaker of the fantastic. Most of the drawings make reference to the idea of motion and were based either on stills from Méliès' films or photographs of him. This drawing (93) shows a woman twirling, her skirt expanding until the entire image is obliterated. The illustration at both corners are tiny movies that work when the pages are flipped. The horse runs and the moon gets smaller. The combination of magician and artist in Méliès fascinates me.

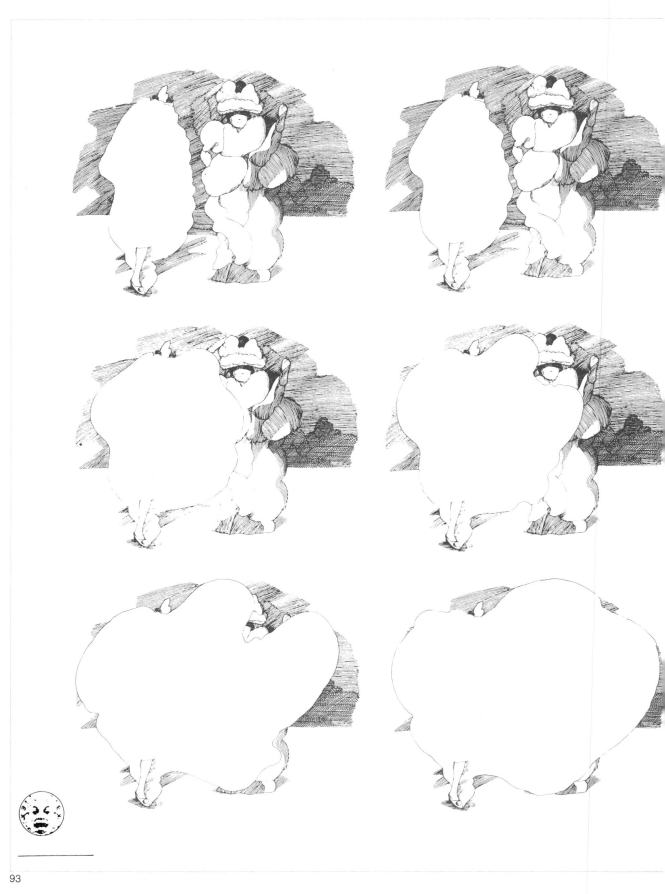

2

GEORGE
MELIES
THE
JULES
VERNE
OF THE
CINEMA
BY
MERRITT
CRAWFORD
CINEMA
THE
MAGAZINE
OF
PHOTOPLAY
OCTOBER
1930

The career of Georges Méliès, aptly described by his countrymen in years past as "le Jules Verne du Cinema," forms an epic in the history of the motion picture, in many respects more amazing, and certainly more tragical than any of the masterpieces of dramatic and fantastic cinematography that for nearly two decades made the name of Méliès and of his productions, Star Films pre-eminent in two hemispheres, wherever motion pictures were shown.

Méliès may be said to have been the first man who really had a true conception of the motion picture as

Motion once again, with
Méliès this time jumping up
and coming down. It seems
rather clumsily drawn to me
now, particularly the way the
arms are done, but the spirit
is nice.

On December 28th, 1895 the Lumière brothers hired the basement of a Paris café from a doubting management, set up their projector, and invited the patrons upstairs to step down and see the show. Thirty-five people paid their francs, trooped downstairs, and became the world's first movie audience. What they saw is now a matter of history; workers leaving a factory, a train arriving at a station (several fainted as the engine approached the camera) and a comedy called *L'Arroseur arrosé*. There was also a film of a bathing belle. "The sea in this picture," wrote an enthusiastic journalist, "is a veritable marvel, so true to life, so wide, so vivid, so moving." When

the audience left at the end of the show one man remained behind. He was Georges Méliès.

Méliès was 34. He came of a wealthy Paris family. He was a jack-of-all-trades, endowed with a vivid imagination and a love of making things with his hands. In his early twenties his manual skill had made him in turn factory worker, mechanic, cabinet-maker and designer. Later he took to painting and caricature. But his principal passion was conjuring. At the age of 26 he bought the Théatre Robert-Houdin in the Passage de l'Opéra. Here he sought to revive the mid-nineteenth century pantomime tradition of Debureau in his own terms. He staged

"des spectacles" such as *La Guirlande Magique* and *Le Tableau de Fantaisie*" in which illusion was the principal attraction. He became producer, actor, scene painter. He built sets out of old bits of three-ply and property swords out of soap-boxes with a rapidity that astonished his colleagues. He rigged up electric circuits for special effects. 'I was an intellectual worker and a manual worker at the same time," he said.

Small wonder then that when he saw his first films Méliès should remain behind when everyone else had gone. Here was a new medium for spectacles, a new way of making magic. "I marvelled at it," he declared. Somehow or other he must

3

MAGICIAN
OF THE
MOVIES
BY
STUART
LEGG
WORLD
FILM
NEWS
MARCH
1938

get hold of the means of making films. "I went up to Lumière and tried to make him sell me his invention. I offered him ten thousand francs, twenty thousand, fifty thousand. I was prepared to offer him my whole fortune, my house, my family possessions." But Lumière would not listen. He said: "Young man, my invention is not for sale, and in any case it would only ruin you. Perhaps for a time it may be exploited as a scientific curiosity, but apart from that it has no commercial future whatever."

This refusal did not count for much with Méliès. The rainy, wobbling films had given him the thrill of his life and he was determined, Lumière or no Lumière, to make films himself. If he could not buy someone else's equipment, then he would make his own. He had designated intricate machines for his theatre and he was a skilled mechanic. Given money, the problems were not insuperable. He came to London and bought film from Paul, the pioneer English producer.

His camera finished, Méliès roamed about shooting anything that interested him. He shot regiments on the march, traffic in the streets, trains arriving and leaving. Then he bethought himself of the acts at his own theatre. One of these was a disappearing woman. It was an act of which Méliès was proud; it drew large audiences, and professionals had failed to discover how it was done. He filmed it under the title of *Escamotage d'une Femme chez Robert-Houdin*. But the film was not a success. "Evidently," said Méliès, "the whole thing appeared childish on the screen. The audience could only see a lot of smoke and flames. They did not get the idea."

Then, in 1896, occurred the celebrated incident which showed Méliès the first secret of trick photography. He was shooting in the Paris streets, using a tripod camera. While he was turning, his camera jammed and stopped. He cleared the jam and continued shooting. When the shot appeared on the screen a bus, which

(96)
I think this is the most successful drawing of the series.
I like the enlarged scale of
Méliès in relationship to the
picture, the implication of
motion that the line around
his head gives, almost as
though he were coming into
focus magically.

was in the centre of the viewfinder
at the moment of the jam, suddenly
turned into a hearse. This was the
clue that Méliès had been subcon-
sciously looking for. He realised that
the cinema did not require magic
thrust upon it as in *Escamotage d'une
Femme*. It could make magic of its
own accord. Three days later he began his first trick film.

Within a short period he had discovered many of the effects we know
to-day. In *Le Manoir du Diable, Le
Cauchemar, Le Cabinet de Méphis-
tophélès, La Vie de Jeanne D'Arc*
and other films made before the turn
of the century he used fast and slow
motion, superimposition, one-turn-
one-picture photography and fades.
In *Orchestre* he made multiple ex-
posures and acted with himself in
the same shot. In another film he
caused a lump of clay to shape itself
into a statue by reversed shooting.
His work became the envy of his
rivals: but Méliès kept his secrets
well, and for several years no one
could guess how his tricks were done.

Until 1897 interior shooting was
unheard of. Film was slow and aper-
tures comparatively small. But in
that year the singer Paulus came to
Méliès and asked to be filmed in
one of his operatic parts. Méliès
agreed, but at the last minute Paulus
refused to undergo the ordeal of appearing in the open air in costume
and make-up. Méliès collected as
much artificial light as he could,
painted a backcloth, placed Paulus
against it, and for the first time in
movie history shot a film indoors. A
few months later he built himself a
studio at Montreuil, "a cross," as he
said, "between a photographer's
studio and a theatre stage." It was
about thirty yards long and twelve
across. At the stage end were a multitude of trap-doors, concealed holes
and movable panels designed to fa-

cilitate the sudden appearances and vanishings of his actors. There were capstans, winches and pulleys to enable the principals to descend from the skies, to float on air and to rise again. The roof was of glass, and though in 1898 he installed electric lamps, Méliès was mainly dependent upon the sun for his lighting. "You have to work fast," he said, "for if you lose time you lose the sun, and then good-bye to shooting."

The studio gave Méliès new opportunities. He was able to combine trick photography and cutting with his own feats of conjuring. His films grew longer, faster in tempo and more complex in action. His output increased until, by 1900, he was making a film a week in addition to three 'superproductions' of 1,500 feet each—*Cendrillon, Petit Chaperon Rouge* and *Barbe Bleu*. A staff of 50 girls was employed in making coloured versions of every film.

"Film-making," he wrote, "offers such a variety of pursuits, demands such a quantity of work of all kinds and claims so sustained an attention that I did not hesitate to proclaim it the most attractive and fascinating of all the arts. The film director uses a bit of everything: dramatics, design, painting, sculpture, architecture, mechanics, manual labour; all are employed in equal doses in this extraordinary profession." Considering that one of the minor production difficulties of the time was the fact that the day's rushes had to be cut into six-foot strips and developed separately, Méliès's statements about sustained attention cannot be regarded as an exaggeration.

From a combination of conjuring and trick photography it was a short step for Méliès to fantastic narrative. Between 1902 and 1906 he produced (among many others) four story films—*Voyage dans la Lune,*

106

Voyage à Travers l'Impossible, Quatre Cents Coups du Diable, and *Le Raid Paris-Monte Carlo in Cinque Heures*—which are generally considered to be his greatest work. In these films reality was banished. It was replaced by a fairy world in which incredible machines, commonplace objects and strange people changed places with increasing acceleration in a whirl of superb colour and movement. In *Quatre Cents Coups du Diablé* clocks vomited demons, people stalked about the ceiling, the Aurora and the Great Bear met in mortal combat, Saturn leapt from his rings, women burst forth from a juggler's umbrella. Méliès was a poet as well as a magician.

He was also, on occasion, a realist. He staged several dramatic reconstructions of contemporary events, and thus anticipated the March of Time by some twenty-five years. Best known of these were *L'Affaire Dreyfus* and *La Couronnement du Roi Edouard VII.* In the latter the king was played by a wine merchant from the Place d'Italie. Edward VII saw it in Paris and was highly gratified.

It was between 1908 and 1910 that Méliès's troubles began. In the early days it had been the custom for producers to sell copies of their films outright to the exhibitors. But as time went on Gaumont, Pathé and other powerful French organisations took to renting instead. Méliès did not follow suit. He spent money liberally (*Voyage dans la Lune* cost some £1,500) and he wanted a quick return to ensure continuity of production. But with the more convenient system of hiring at their disposal, exhibitors would no longer buy. Competition increased as a result of the American production boom of 1908. Rival French firms discovered Méliès's secrets and imitated them. Gradually his clientèle fell away.

For some years he continued producing. In 1912 came *La Conquête du Pole,* with Father Pole, bearded and terrible, devouring a party of explorers. During the War he made fairy stories for children; *La Fée Libellule, Le Lac Enchanté, La Bonne Bergère et La Mauvaise Princesse* and others. But the star system was rising; the entertainment demands of war were not attuned to fairy tales; the cinema was settling into mass production and the forms of familiar convention.

In 1914 the offices of Méliès's company were commandeered by the military. An almost complete set of copies of his films, covering twenty years of his work, were on the premises. But to move them, to rent a new office and equip new vaults would have cost more than Méliès could now afford. He sold his films to a junk merchant who resold them as industrial celluloid.

For many years Méliès was no more seen. In 1928 someone recognized him in the streets of Paris. He was selling newspapers. His friends got up a subscription to buy him a tobacco kiosk near the Gare St. Lazare. When he became too old to sell cigarettes and sweets the Chambre Syndicale Française du Cinématographe, which he founded in 1897 and of which he was president for ten years, arranged for him to live in the Maison de Retraite d'Orly, a home for destitute actors. "I have been in retirement here for three years," he wrote in 1936 to an English director. "Being the dean of cinematographers (the first one after Lumière) I am an old man, 75 years old; and since I want to stay on earth as long as possible I have to take precautions." On January 22nd, 1938, he died of cancer. The expenses of his funeral were defrayed by French and English film workers.

(98-103)
This children's book *Cats and Bats and Things with Wings* was created in collaboration with the American poet, Conrad Aiken. We reversed the customary working procedure between writer and artist. I sent a drawing first to Aiken; within a week he wrote a poem to it. This system worked very well, although one can see why it might not always be practical. My graphic idea was to do every drawing in a different style, a kind of muscle flexing. I used a very rigid format to give the book continuity since the drawings didn't.

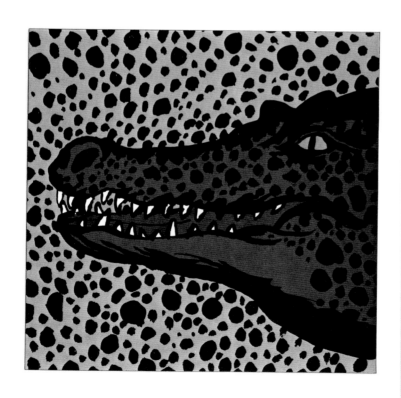

The Crocodile.

O crocodile
that ancient smile
old as the Congo
or the Nile
and full of wile
and full of guile
o crocodile
dear crocodile
ARE you mayhap
a tourist trap
ready to snap
at you
or me
and
TAKE
US
KINDLY
IN
TO
TEA?
Is there a tooth behind that smile
are we
to be
the tea?
Yet handsome he
and what a tail
and he can swing it
like a flail
hoping
of course
to knock us flat:
and, if he does,
that's THAT.
O you're a scalawag
scale-awag scalawag
tail-awag scalawag
that's what you are
that's what!

The Seal.

How must it feel
to be
a
seal
and swish among the
ducks
and teal
and swim
a cool
Virginia Reel
right underneath
somebody's
keel?
Then
much
to
somebody's surprise
pop up your head
right out of sea
and blink your big blue baby eyes
and flap your fins
with glee?
And o what bliss
on summer days
what bliss it is
to lie and laze
on a warm mudflat
in the sun
and *sunbathe*
just
like
anyone.
I think the seal
has
all
the
fun.

The Fallow Deer.

The fallow deer
how lovely he
with horns
just like
a Christmas Tree
that is
if you put
spangles on
and tinsel on
and bangles on
and he's as gentle
as can be
so meek
so mild
that any child
can feed him with her hand
and stand
and stare
he doesn't
care.
You ask me
why they call him
fallow
it is because
he's
kind of yallow
when he is young
he has a dapple
and
o
my
how
he
loves
an
apple.

The elephant grows very old
he lives to years untold
and as you see he's *mani*fold:
with folds and folds of rubbery skin
some tucked out and some tucked in
his eye
is shy
and he is humorous and sly.
And o my how he loves a tub
and someone with a brush to scrub
those folds and kinks
and clean
his toes and all that's in between
while with his trunk he drinks
and sprays his back and *winks*.
Then when the bath is done
he thinks it's fun
to dunk
his trunk
and squirt his back all over
with dust and straws and clover.
Old elephant is clever:
he never
forgets:
but lets
something he sees stay in his mind
while years and years unwind:
if someone is unkind
he'll find
a way to punish the unkind one.
But to the *kind* one
he'll go down on his knees
as if to say
I don't forget that day
long ago and far away
when you were good to me:
my memory never ends:
let us be friends.

The Elephant.

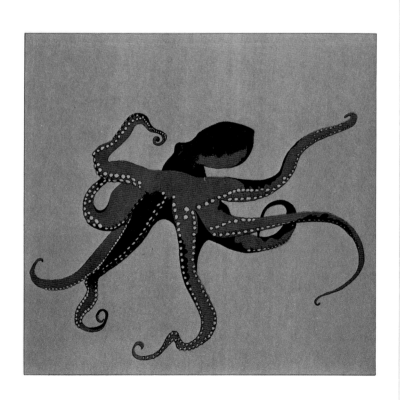

The many-handed octopus
does not INTEND to frighten us:
his family name is octopod
and certainly he is odd.
A kind of spider of the sea
is he.
Lovely to watch him waver round
under the sea without a sound
and how he folds
            and then unfolds
                  shapes
                     and then reshapes
                        drapes
                           and then undrapes
each slithery arm and hand
and
still always can
come back to where he first began.
O what a juggler he could be:
the greatest juggler of the sea:
eight balls at once he'd keep with ease
above his head beneath the seas
passing from one to other
without the slightest bother.
But if WE frighten HIM
then suddenly all goes dim
behind a cloud of ink
he seems to shrink
and off unseen he'll swiftly swim
upon a pearly oyster bed
to lay his troubled head.

The Octopus.

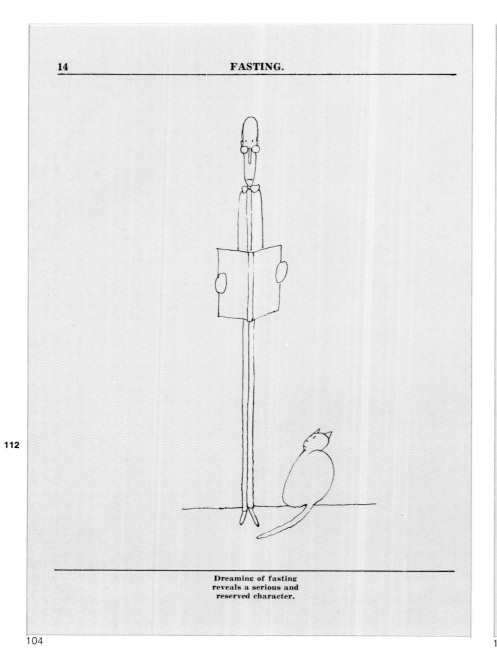

Dreaming of fasting
reveals a serious and
reserved character.

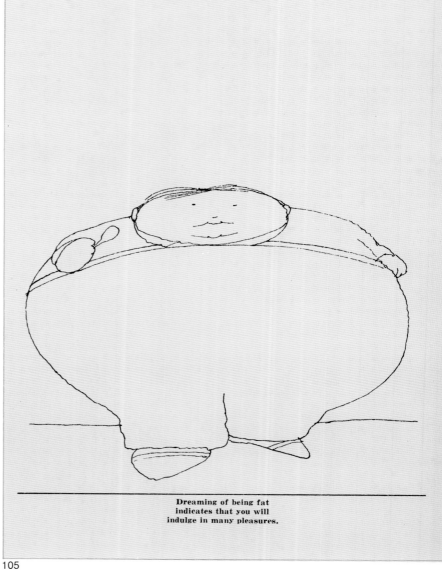

Dreaming of being fat
indicates that you will
indulge in many pleasures.

(104-107)
A selection of pages from a
Graphic which parodied
books with dream interpreta-
tions. My teacher in Bologna,
Giorgio Morandi, taught only
hard ground etching with a
needle, perhaps the most
fundamental way of drawing
outside of using a stick in
sand-just a single un-
weighted, untextured line
incised into a metal plate.
I've never gotten over my
surprise at the expressive
capacity of such a simple
technique.

Dreaming of a dog
signifies trustworthy companions
and fruitful matrimony.

If a lover dreams of
various animals it signifies
that he will soon wed.

(108)
Two characters in a Tennessee Williams play published in *Esquire* were the subject matter of this drawing. Like many of Williams' themes, this one concerned the distortion and mutilation that occurs in human relationships. I tried to create a visual equivalent for that idea by distorting the drawing quality. The horizontal line screen gives the drawing a different textural quality from the original wash drawing. Again, this effect could not have been achieved without employing printing and photoengraving technology.

108

he author ended a series of poems with his original image: a fish in the sky. I emphasized certain aspects of the text by ''overlapping'' the illustrations for this children's book, almost a miniature film moving from scene to scene.

The sequence begins with:

. A fish in the sky, a sailboat below in the water.

. The image of the sail repeated this time in a strange floating ball; the fish-bird flying away in the distance.

. The mysterious ball seen through the window of a room containing a floating flower.

. The flower reappears, crushed among fallen autumn leaves and a child's feet.

. A leaf appears in the form of a raft for an ant.

. The ant on a beach, a jar of plum-colored balls in the foreground, a series of shells in the background.

. Vantage points shift: a shell in the foreground, the jar in the background. The shell contains a listening ear.

. The ear appears inside the window of a barn at night.

. The barn window floats through the air reflecting the moon.

. The moon spotlights a breaking branch on a tree.

. The tree with a road running beside it, seen from inside a cave.

. The road is closer, a giant foot in the foreground.

. The road replaced by a river, a glass of fog on its bank.

. The original fish in the sky appears, flying above the river, completing the cycle.

Throughout the book, each illustration foreshadows later images while continuing images from previous illustrations.

A

B

a May fly singing above the brook
is not just a twilight song,
it's a field flower floating
in an empty room...

C

a pebble is not just a pebble washed
in from the sea, it's a seadrop like a
raindrop the color of a plum to put into
an old peach jar...

F

a walk in the woods when the leaves
have turned is not just
being alone, it's the smell of
earth and sky and twigs cracking under your
feet, and not going too far because you promised
you wouldn't...

D

a shell tossed on the bone-bleached
shore is not just a chamber of whispering
song, it's a seaflower's ear listening
to you...

G

a leaf fallen from a tree is not
just a leaf fallen from a tree, it's a
raft to put to sea an ant or two and
wishing you were sailor three...

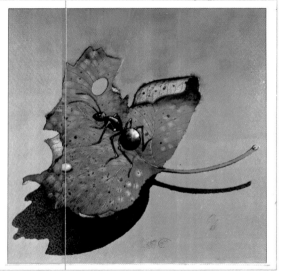

E

a clapboard barn with rippled dark
windowpanes is not just for looking
into, it's for listening to—like a
gravestone without a name...

H

darkness is not just darkness,
it's invisible raindrops wind-whipped
against your windowpane, it's the creak
of the floor or an opening door...
it's holding your pillow tight when
you're falling through the night...

I

a road is not just a road,
bags packed to go to sea,
it's as if it had something to say to a boy
other than crickets and hoppers and little rocks
to kick off the planet with your toe...

L

a branch broken from a birch tree
is not just a branch broken from a birch
tree, it's a branch that will never grow again
another silvery leaf...

J

an old covered bridge crossing
the still-deeps is not just a bridge
under the dark, it's the murmuring of
mist men gathered for a smoke and a
glass of fog...

M

117

a cave is not just a cave, it's
like you're always reaching into your
pocket when you know there's nothing
there...

K

a rocky brook is not just looking
down, it's looking up—clouds of clouds,
leafy minnows, fish in the sky...

N

This sequence of photos was inspired by the title of the record album it was done for, "Don Randi Trio + 1 at the Baked Potato." As is very often the case, the music was not available for listening until after the deadline for the album cover was past. Because I had no idea of the musical content I chose to work off the title (a desperate but frequently resorted-to solution).
The Baked Potato turns out to be a night club where the performance was recorded. I did a small painting of a burning baked potato which I set on fire with instructions to the photographer to record every stage of the conflagration. I used the second and final picture for the front (112) and back (111) of the album.

118

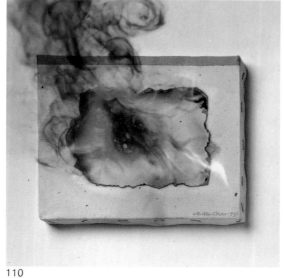

SIDE ONE

1.
TUBESTEAK
Don Randi
Donaway Music
BMI. 3.25

2.
THERE IS NO
GREATER LOVE
Marty Symes
Isham Jones
World Music
Inc. ASCAP
3.50

3.
"EVERYBODY'S
TALKIN'"
"Fred Neil
Third Story
Music Inc.
BMI. 3.22

4.
SPACE ODYSSEY,
THUS SPAKE
ZARATHUSTRA
Richard Strauss
Henmar Press
Inc. ASCAP
BLUE DANUBE
Johann Strauss
P.D. 6.30

MUSICIANS:
DON RANDI,
PIANO
JOHN SUMMER,
DRUMS
HAL GORDON,
CONGA
HARVEY NEWMARK,
BASS

SIDE TWO:

1.
I FOUND GOLD
Don Randi
Donaway Music
BMI. 2.32

2.
MERCY MERCY
Josef Zawinul
Zawinul Music
BMI. 3.35

3.
SAMBA DE ORFEO
Louis Bonfa
Ann Rachel M.
ASCAP 3.50

4.
I'LL BE THERE
Bob West,
Hal Davis,
Willie Hutch,
Berry Gordy,
Jobete Music
Co., Inc.
BMI. 3.10

5.
LEAH ROSE
Don Randi
Donaway Music
BMI. 3.00

CREDITS:

PRODUCED BY:
DON RANDI
ARRANGED BY:
DON RANDI
RECORDED LIVE
AT THE
BAKED POTATO
BY DELTA SOUND
RECORDING
ENGINEER:
JERRY BARNES

DESIGNED BY MILTON GLASER, PHOTOGRAPHED BY PEGGY BARNETT

111

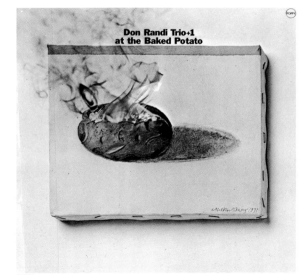

112

119

Simon's Palette, torn apart   Milton Glaser July 6, 66

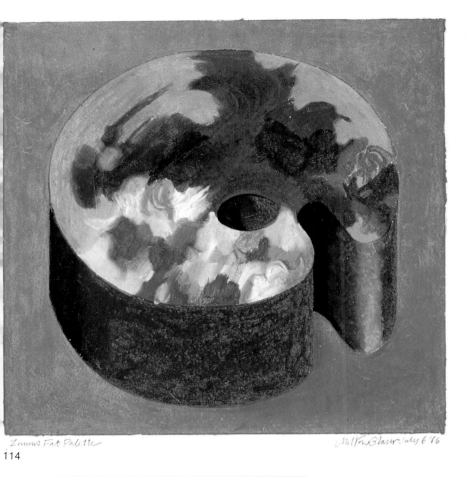

Zimm's Fat Palette   Milton Glaser July 6 '66

114

Zimm's Palette, M's Fingers   Milton Glaser July 4 '66

115

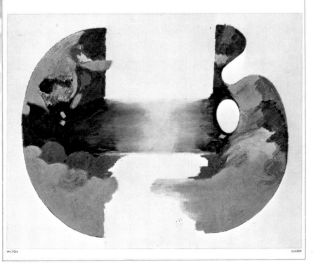

116

(113-116)
In 1962 I bought a house in the country, in Woodstock, New York. Its former owner was a sculptor named Bruno Zimm. It's a wonderful house and his presence is still very much there, although he died in 1945. His palette continues to hang on the studio wall. I did a series of crayon drawings of it; one of them, torn apart, was used by *Graphis*, the great Swiss magazine serving an international design community, as a cover (116). For that purpose I also tore the lettering apart. This would have been an extremely tough solution to justify for any other magazine, since most logos are considered sacred.

(117-121)
These drawings illustrated
an article on amphetamine
abuse for *New York*. As in
Fish in the Sky, I was
attempting a kind of miniature
film. The illustrations ran
consecutively over five pages
which contributed to the
movie effect.

117

118

119

120

(122)
Often typography is the main or only graphic element in a design. This is a common solution when the subject matter is too broad or complex to be expressed with a single specific image. Letterforms are inherently more abstract than pictures, consequently more useful for this kind of problem. It is also possible for letterforms to develop a decidedly illustrative quality, as some of the examples on the following pages indicate. For this dust jacket, I tried to design letterforms that in some way looked like the words sounded. To intensify the unusual quality of this book, the author's name, customarily appearing on the front, was moved to the back with lettering same size and style.

124

The Underground Gourmet

$1.95

Where to find great meals in New York for less than $2.00 and as little as 50¢.

BY MILTON GLASER AND JEROME SNYDER

(123)
Jerome Snyder and I wrote this book on the subject of good cheap restaurants in New York. I set the title in an alphabet designed by Seymour Chwast called Artone. I used the U and the G as a basis for a trademark, taking advantage of their unusual shape. In New York more people know me as a food writer than as a designer. I find that somewhat depressing.

STEREO 101

MILTON GLASER

This poster sought to reflect
the spectrum of a radio
station's music, as well as
the range of its audience.
It is not entirely successful,
but I like parts of it. The type
is Neo-Futura, my stencil
variation of the classic
Bauhaus Futura type face.
I was surprised that the type
reads as well as it does, in
spite of the visual interruption
in the letterforms.

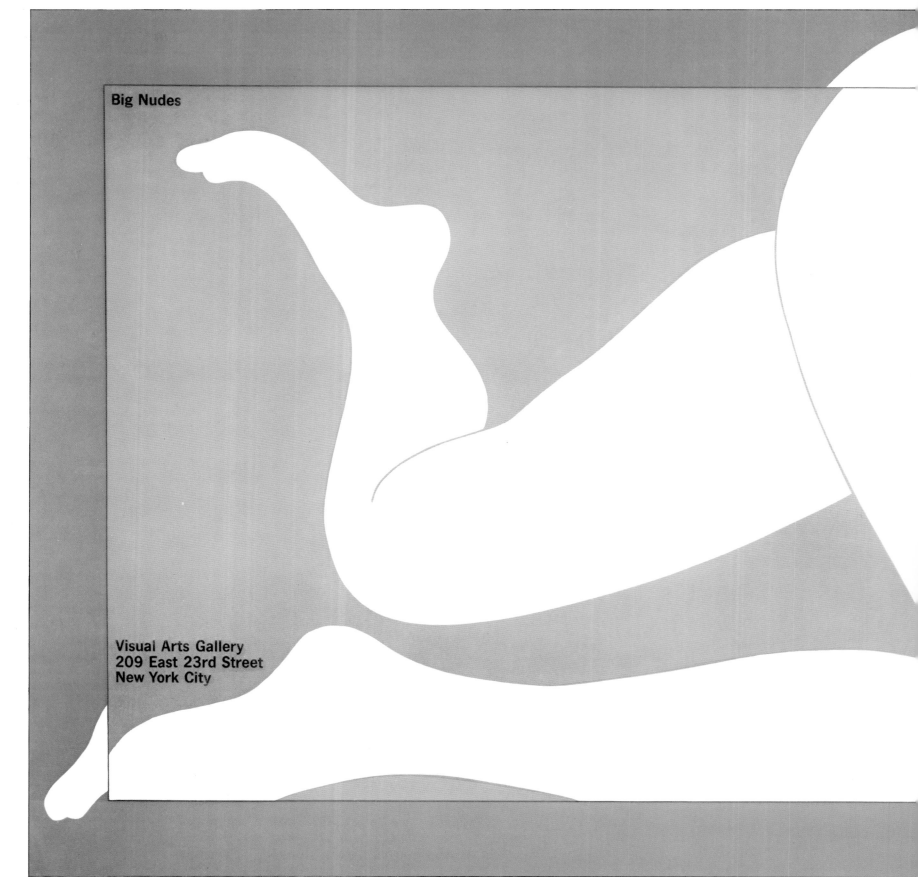

Big Nudes

Visual Arts Gallery
209 East 23rd Street
New York City

(125)
Excepting the Dylan poster, this School of Visual Arts poster announcing a show of paintings of large nudes, seems to be my best known work. The graphic idea was to show a nude so large it couldn't fit on the page, extending therefore into the space behind. Later I did a large silkscreen of the same drawing which continues to sell like hot cakes.

(126)
My typography on this poster
is rather clumsy, but the two
B's with the profiles of
Brubeck and Basie have a
certain vigor.

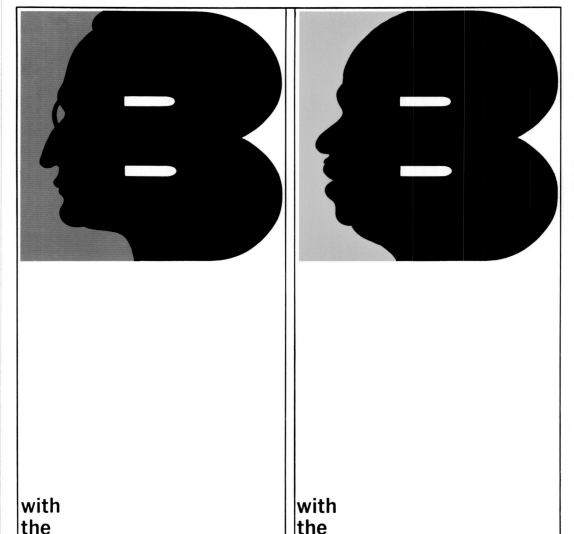

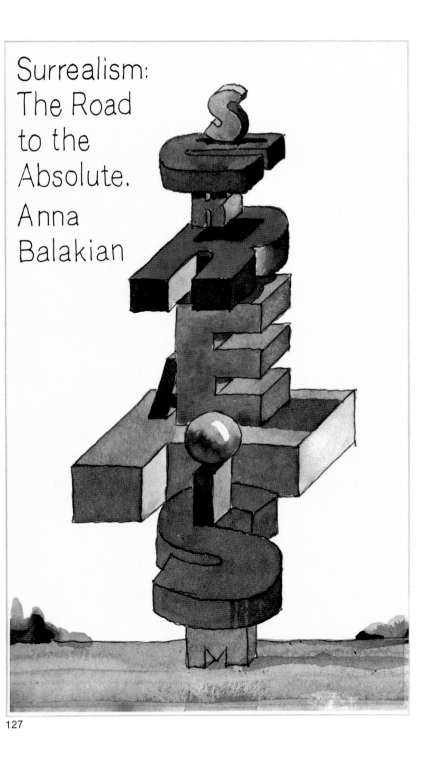

Surrealism:
The Road
to the
Absolute.
Anna
Balakian

Here's one that got away. This sketch was done for a paperback on surrealism. The author hated it and it was rejected. (Usually, authors do not have approval of cover art which drives many of them crazy.) Announcements for art exhibitions or covers for books about art are very problematical; the designer imposes his vision or, more accurately, superimposes his vision on an already existing visual frame of reference. This is all very delicate. The most common solution is to simply reproduce an example of the art work, although this frequently yields uninteresting results.

132

95c

JOHN DICKSON

First of
the famous
Dr. Gideon Fell
mysteries

CARR

Hag's Nook

MILTON GLASER

128

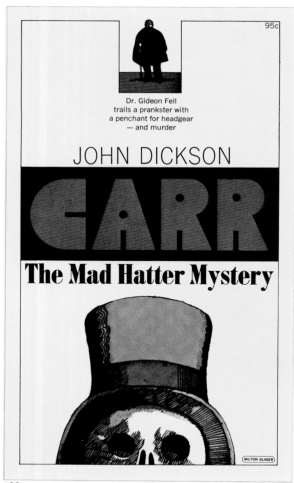

95c

JOHN DICKSON

Dr. Gideon Fell
trails a prankster with
a penchant for headgear
— and murder

CARR

The Mad Hatter Mystery

MILTON GLASER

129

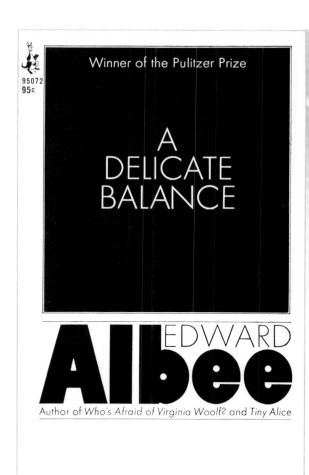

95072
95c

Winner of the Pulitzer Prize

A
DELICATE
BALANCE

EDWARD
Albee

Author of *Who's Afraid of Virginia Woolf?* and *Tiny Alice*

130

(128, 129)
This pair of paperback covers
falters somewhat because of
their informational burden.
The drawing of the hero, the
description of the book's
content, the identification of
a famous author, the book's
title, and an image relating
to the content—not to
mention the price and my
name—is asking a bit much
of a four by seven surface.
Nice try, but no cigar.

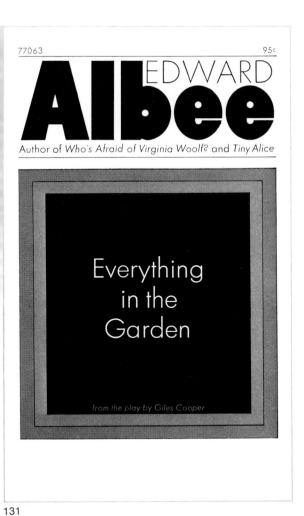

77063
95¢

EDWARD
Albee

Author of *Who's Afraid of Virginia Woolf?* and *Tiny Alice*

Everything
in the
Garden

from the play by Giles Cooper

131

PN224/95¢
AVON
CLASSIC CRIME
COLLECTION

Mary Kelly

A stubborn young man asks a guilty town
one too many questions about violent death . . .

Dead Corse

The first appearance in paperback of
one of the great suspense writers of our time!

132

PN294/95¢
AVON
CLASSIC CRIME
COLLECTION

Michael Innes

A unique suspense novelist's most chilling tale

One Man Show

A gallery of spies and counterspies,
artists and art thieves, their portraits painted in blood

133

133

(130-133)
The two Albee covers work
in series, but I ran the risk,
without the help of a
distinguishing illustration,
of the reader thinking he had
read the book before. For
the Avon Classic Crime
Collection I developed a
format (132) that emphasized
the series identification
even though different illustrators were to be used.
Roger Hane illustrated many
of them brilliantly (133).

(134, 135)
A similar graphic device for wholly different books: the idea of combining the letterform with the image of teeth. When I am taken with an idea, I find it difficult not to use it again (and again sometimes) although with variations, of course.

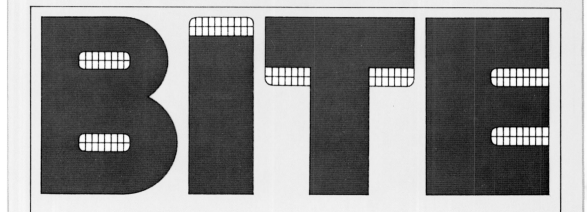

BITE

A

NEW YORK

RESTAURANT STRATEGY

FOR HEDONISTS,
MASOCHISTS, SELECTIVE
PENNY PINCHERS AND THE
UPWARDLY MOBILE

GAEL GREENE

THE INSATIABLE CRITIC

Knut Hamsun

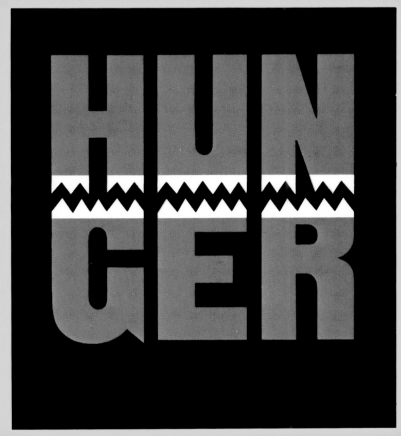

A new translation by Robert Bly
with an introduction by Isaac Bashevis Singer

NOONDAY 302 $2.25

The Chocolate Deal
A Novel
Haim Gouri

MILTON GLASER

(136)
A book jacket with a symbol implicit in the title. Something happens when the power and terror of the swastika is translated into chocolate. The story concerned German reparations to the Jews after the war.

(137)
A promotional brochure for a film was the commission. I knew very little about the movie except that some bloody sequences about pig killing were central to the plot. In an oblique way I used that as my subject. If you are showing pigs being killed, this is a rather graceful way of doing it. The motion picture didn't do well and I was never paid for the job. So it goes.

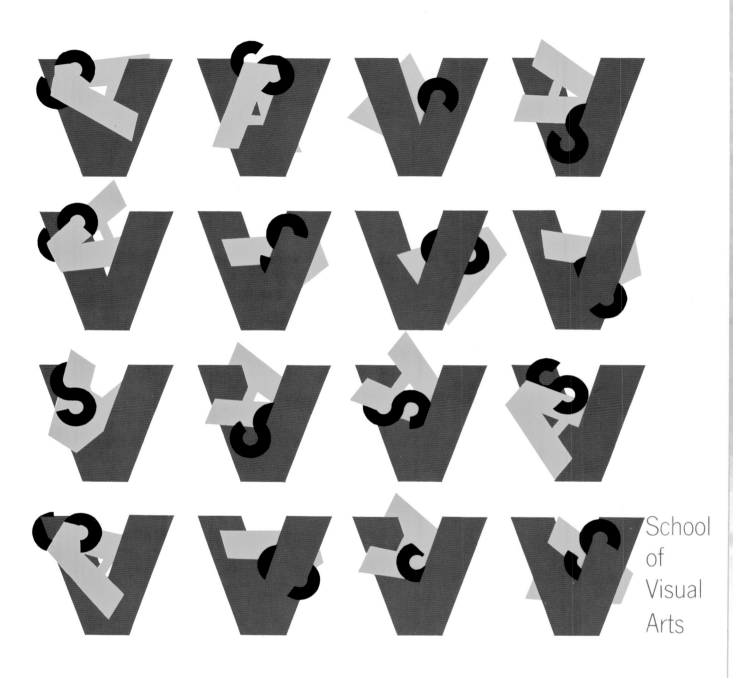

School
of
Visual
Arts

(138)
Designing a cover for an art school catalog is a similar problem to designing art show announcements; in this instance, to suggest the spirit and substance of a school embracing a multitude of styles—I aimed for a sense of activity, flexibility, and a contemporary spirit.

(139)
The publisher described *GOG* as a big book about a big man. I attempted to convey that idea by wrapping the word around the spine and across the front to suggest a subject too large to be confined by the limitations of the page. I had apprehensions about this solution. When a book is badly produced, the spine creeps to the front, or the title creeps spinewards. Did some people think the jacket was an accident of production rather than an intentional effect?

(140)
Conrad's great book gave me a sense of compression and density which led me to design these bulky, compressed letterforms. The image of a knotted rope amplifies that sense and also introduces a sailing reference.

140

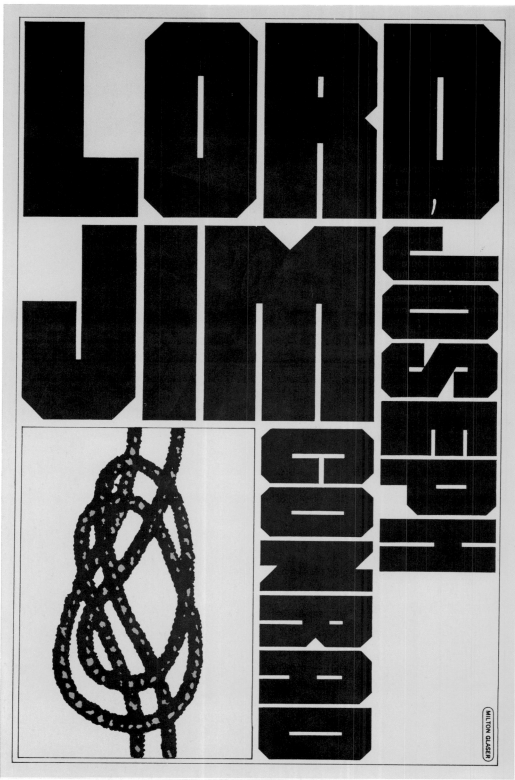

HOLIDAY

NOVEMBER 1967 · 75c

THE SUN VALLEY SET
BY STEPHEN BIRMINGHAM

INTERLUDE IN BUDAPEST
BY LILLIAN HELLMAN

THE BOUTIQUES OF PARIS AND ROME
BY EUGENIA SHEPPARD

BEAUTIFUL, BUSYBODY BERMUDA
BY ALFRED BESTER

THE FINEST FOOD OF FRANCE
BY SILAS SPITZER

MILTON GLASER

(141)
A deliberate *art nouveau* knock-off done for *Holiday* when the magazine's format was still large. This cover was extremely effective in black and white because it stood out from the other magazines with their full color covers on the newsstand. For a designer, context is everything.

(142-145)
The following eight pages
comprise a series of
announcements I designed
for the School of Visual Arts
Gallery. The theme uniting
the examples on this spread
has to do with the passage
of time. (142, 144) concern
two separate shows that ran
consecutively. (142) was on
California Painting. I tried
to suggest the qualities of
that painting style by invent-
ing a slick mechanical-
looking number one. A
strange-looking hairy object
is beginning to intrude. For
the second exhibition (144),
the "number one" departs
and the hairy "number two"
moves in. The quality and
shape of the two is an
attempt to evoke the Chicago
style of painting that made
up the show. Combining the
ideas of an opening and a
magazine (143) led me to a
solution which shows a page
being turned and the word
"TWEN" being revealed.
Another attempt to express
time on a flat surface is the
image of an apple turning in
space (145). This solution
depends on a bit of colloquial
142 understanding: The title of
the show was "Inside the
Big Apple," the Big Apple
being a term for New York
City. The exhibition consisted
of paintings of New York
interiors. Without an understanding of the expression,
the whole job falls apart,
but the New York audience
for whom these announce-
ments were intended would
obviously understand it and
consequently the risk was
minimal.

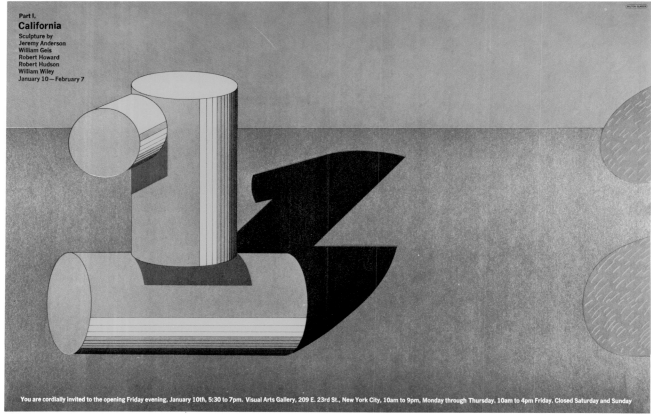

Part I,
California
Sculpture by
Jeremy Anderson
William Geis
Robert Howard
Robert Hudson
William Wiley
January 10—February 7

You are cordially invited to the opening Friday evening, January 10th, 5:30 to 7pm. Visual Arts Gallery, 209 E. 23rd St., New York City, 10am to 9pm, Monday through Thursday. 10am to 4pm Friday. Closed Saturday and Sunday

142

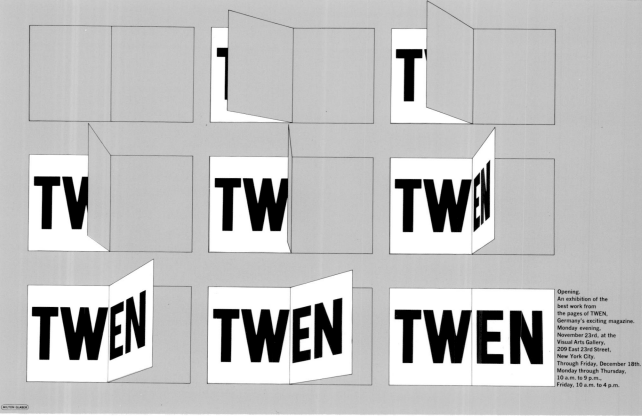

Opening.
An exhibition of the
best work from
the pages of TWEN,
Germany's exciting magazine.
Monday evening,
November 23rd, at the
Visual Arts Gallery,
209 East 23rd Street,
New York City.
Through Friday, December 18th.
Monday through Thursday,
10 a.m. to 9 p.m.,
Friday, 10 a.m. to 4 p.m.

143

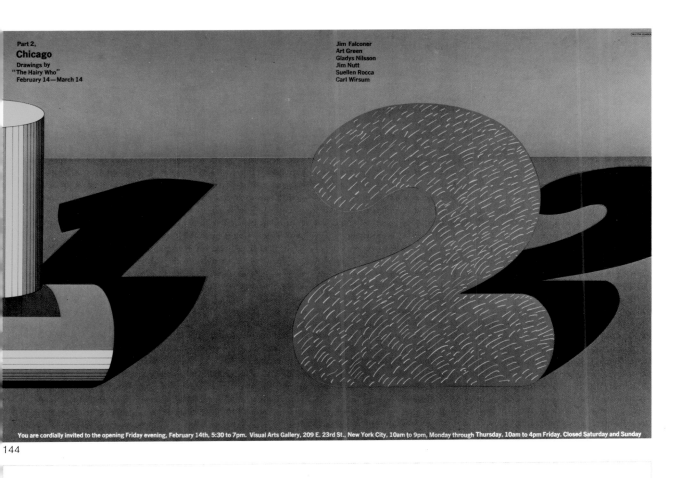

Part 2,
Chicago
Drawings by
"The Hairy Who"
February 14—March 14

Jim Falconer
Art Green
Gladys Nilsson
Jim Nutt
Suellen Rocca
Carl Wirsum

You are cordially invited to the opening Friday evening, February 14th, 5:30 to 7pm. Visual Arts Gallery, 209 E. 23rd St., New York City, 10am to 9pm, Monday through Thursday. 10am to 4pm Friday. Closed Saturday and Sunday

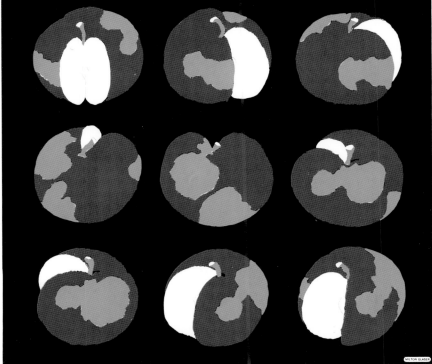

Inside
The Big
Apple

Paintings
of
New York
Interiors

Herb Katzman
Alex Katz
Sylvia Mangold
Howard Kanovitz
John Koch
Malcolm Morley
Jack Beal
Robert De Niro
Richard Artschw
Lowell Nesbitt
Arakawa

October 8th to
November 1st
Monday to Thursday
10 am to 9 pm
Friday 10 am to 4 pm
Closed Saturday
and Sunday

You are cordially
invited to
the opening
Monday evening
October 8th,
5 to 7 pm.
Visual Arts Gallery
209 East 23rd Street
New York City

MILTON GLASER

(146-149)
The painting of Whistler's mother (146) was rendered in two different styles to announce a show of single works of art created by two people. The show was interesting although the idea didn't exactly sweep the art world. The poison pen (147) was created for a show of satirical drawings by a group of excellent cartoonists and illustrators; the other announcements on this spread were done for a graphic design show in Milan (148); a survey of contemporary landscape paintings (149).

(150-153)
A selection of one painting and one print by a variety of artists (150); a show of concrete poetry (151); graphic work produced under the aegis of Robert Delpire—how to change R into D (152); and an announcement for Stanley VanDerBeek (153), a good friend who is a filmmaker and artist. All the examples on this spread use letterforms in an illustrative way to achieve their impact.

144

Combine Works

April 8th to
May 7th
Monday to Thursday
10 am to 9 pm
Friday 10 am to 4 pm
Closed Saturday
and Sunday

You are cordially
invited to the opening
Tuesday, April 8th
5:30 to 7pm.
Visual Arts Gallery
209 East 23rd Street
New York City

Ray Johnson & May Wilson
Ray Johnson & Ero Lippold
Ray Johnson & John Willenbecher
Ray Johnson & Richard C.
Will Insley & Kent English
Frank Roth & Malcolm Morley
Joseph Raffael & Ray Johnson
Joseph Raffael & William T. Wiley
Joseph Raffael & Bruce Nauman
Robyn Martin & Arlo Acton
  & Giovanni Ragusa
Edwin Ruda & Robert Huot
Clay Spohn & John Speorri
Don Nice & Joseph Zucker
William T. Wiley & William Geis
James Rosenquist & Harry Soviak
Victor Kotowitz & Emil Mare
Wolf Kahn & Milton Glaser
Richard Van Buren & Rex Lau
Hans Dorflinger & Gills Larrain

146

The Poison Pen

Viperous drawings by
R. O. Blechman
William Charmatz
Seymour Chwast
Jules Feiffer
Jean Michel Folon
David Levine
Jerome Snyder
Edward Sorel
Roland Topor
Tomi Ungerer

Friday,
November 19th through
Friday,
December 17th
The Visual Arts Gallery
209 East 23rd Street
New York City
Monday through
Thursday
10 a.m. to 9 p.m.
Friday, 10 a.m. to 4 p.m.

147

MILTON GLASER

Milanese Graphics
Tuesday evening
April 20th through
Tuesday, May 4th
The Visual Arts Gallery
209 East 23rd Street
New York City
Monday through
Thursday
10 a.m. to 9 p.m.
Friday 10 a.m.
to 4 p.m.

Antonio Boggeri   Umberto Capelli   Giulio Confalonieri   Franco Grignani   Giancarlo Iliprandi   Giovanni Pintori   & Esempi da Imago

148

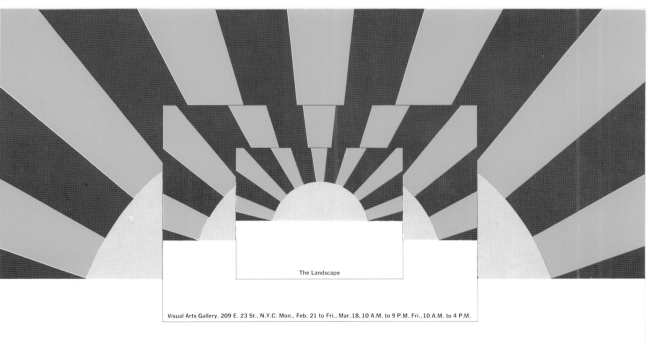

The Landscape

Visual Arts Gallery, 209 E. 23 St., N.Y.C. Mon., Feb. 21 to Fri., Mar. 18, 10 A.M. to 9 P.M. Fri., 10 A.M. to 4 P.M.

Participants:
Sally Amster
Billy Apple
John Bageris
Rudolf Baranik
Rosemarie Beck
Gandy Brodie
Daniel Brustlein
Lawrence Calcagno

Gretna Campbell
Carmen Cicero
William Clutz
Barry Cohen
Allan D'Arcangelo
Elaine de Kooning
Harvey Dinnerstein
Louis Donato
Nancy Ellison

Akiba Emanuel
Mario Fallani
Louis Finkelstein
Miles Forst
Mary Frank
Robert Frankenberg
Ann Freilich
Jane Freilicher
Howard Fussiner

Richard Gangel
Paul Georges
Edward Giobbi
Joel Goldblatt
Leon Goldin
Gloria Greenberg Bressler
John Grillo
Burt Hasen
Philip Hays

Sophia Healy
Peter Heinemann
John Heliker
Wolf Kahn
Herbert Kallem
Eugene Karlin
Alex Katz
Herbert Katzman
Kenneth Kilstrom

Chaim Koppelman
Stan Landsman
Fay Lansner
Michael Loew
David Lund
Marcia Marcus
Emily Mason
James Mellon
Frank Metz

George Muller
Emily Nelligan
Barbara Nessim
Don Nice
Kathleen O'Toole
Peter Paone
Robert Andrew Parker
Bernard Pfriem
Reginald Pollack

Robert Rabinowitz
Wallace Reiss
Paul Resika
Arthur Rosenbaum
Bernard Rosenquit
Frank Roth
Peter Ruta
Maynard Sandol
W. Lee Savage

David Sawin
Daniel Schwartz
Seymour Shapiro
Morris Shulman
Jack Sonenberg
Anita Steckel
Jordan Steckel
May Stevens
Marius Sznajderman

Louis Tytell
Stanley Vanderbeek
Tony Vevers
E. B. Walden
Robert Weaver
Tom Wesselmann
Jane Wilson
Agatha Wojciechowsky
Adja Yunkers

149

146

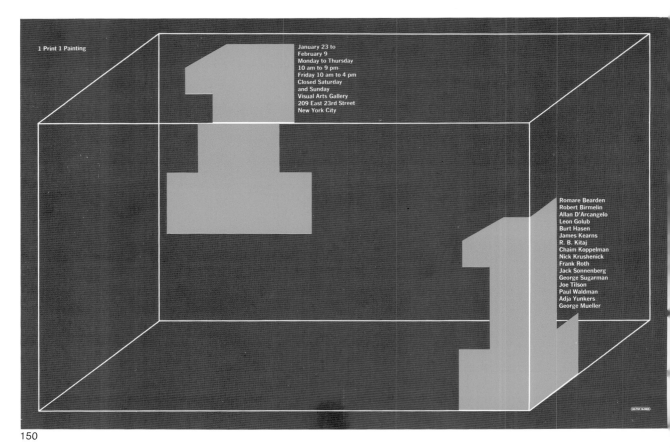

1 Print 1 Painting

January 23 to
February 9
Monday to Thursday
10 am to 9 pm
Friday 10 am to 4 pm
Closed Saturday
and Sunday
Visual Arts Gallery
209 East 23rd Street
New York City

Romare Bearden
Robert Birmelin
Allan D'Arcangelo
Leon Golub
Burt Hasen
James Kearns
R. B. Kitaj
Chaim Koppelman
Nick Krushenick
Frank Roth
Jack Sonnenberg
George Sugarman
Joe Tilson
Paul Waldman
Adja Yunkers
George Mueller

150

CONCRETE
POETRY

Closed evenings, April 9-12

151

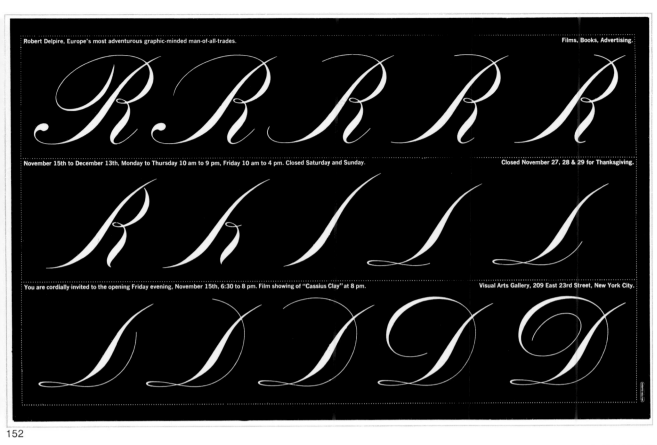

Robert Delpire, Europe's most adventurous graphic-minded man-of-all-trades.

Films, Books, Advertising.

November 15th to December 13th, Monday to Thursday 10 am to 9 pm, Friday 10 am to 4 pm. Closed Saturday and Sunday.

Closed November 27, 28 & 29 for Thanksgiving.

You are cordially invited to the opening Friday evening, November 15th, 6:30 to 8 pm. Film showing of "Cassius Clay" at 8 pm.

Visual Arts Gallery, 209 East 23rd Street, New York City.

152

Films,   calligraphy,   stills   paintings,   polaroids,   sculpture,   rollings,   wooden boxes,   and   collages.

The World of Stanley VanDerBeek   The Visual Arts Gallery   209 East 23rd Street   New York City   Tuesday, March 29th to Friday, April 22nd   Monday through Thursday 10 a.m. to 9 p.m.   Friday, 10 a.m. to 4 p.m

153

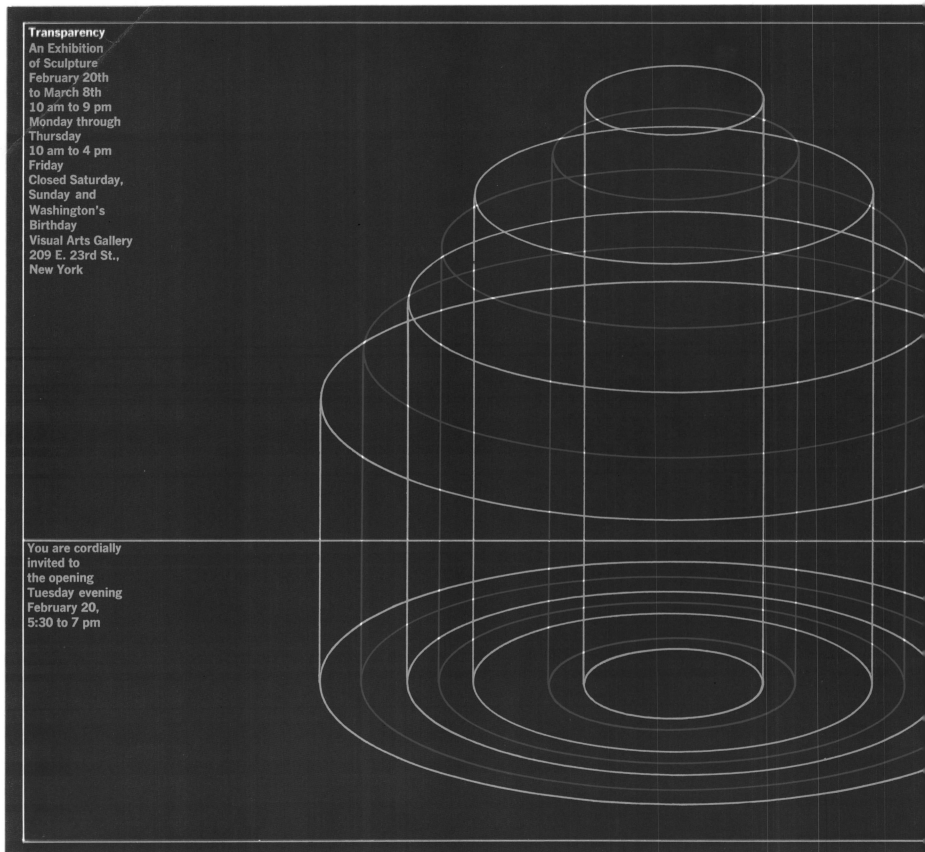

Transparency
An Exhibition
of Sculpture
February 20th
to March 8th
10 am to 9 pm
Monday through
Thursday
10 am to 4 pm
Friday
Closed Saturday,
Sunday and
Washington's
Birthday
Visual Arts Gallery
209 E. 23rd St.,
New York

You are cordially
invited to
the opening
Tuesday evening
February 20,
5:30 to 7 pm

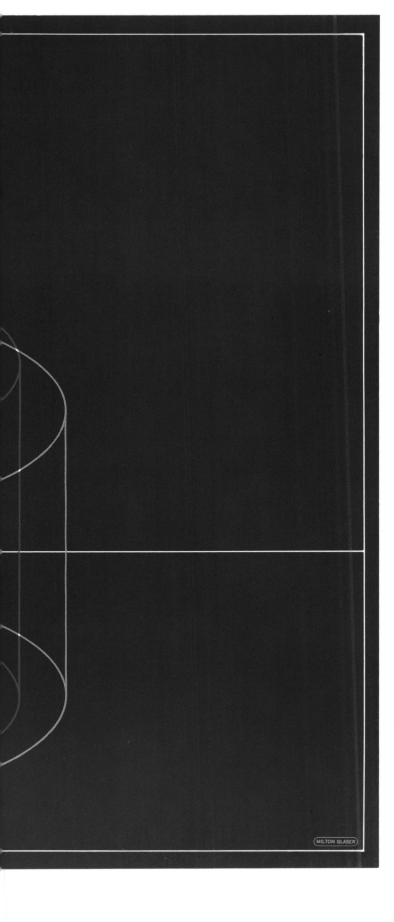

149

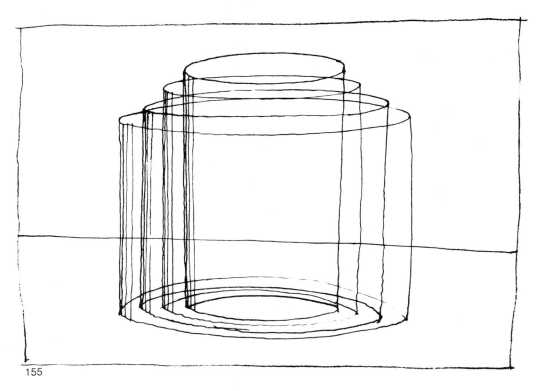

155

Journal of The American Institute of Graphic Arts

5

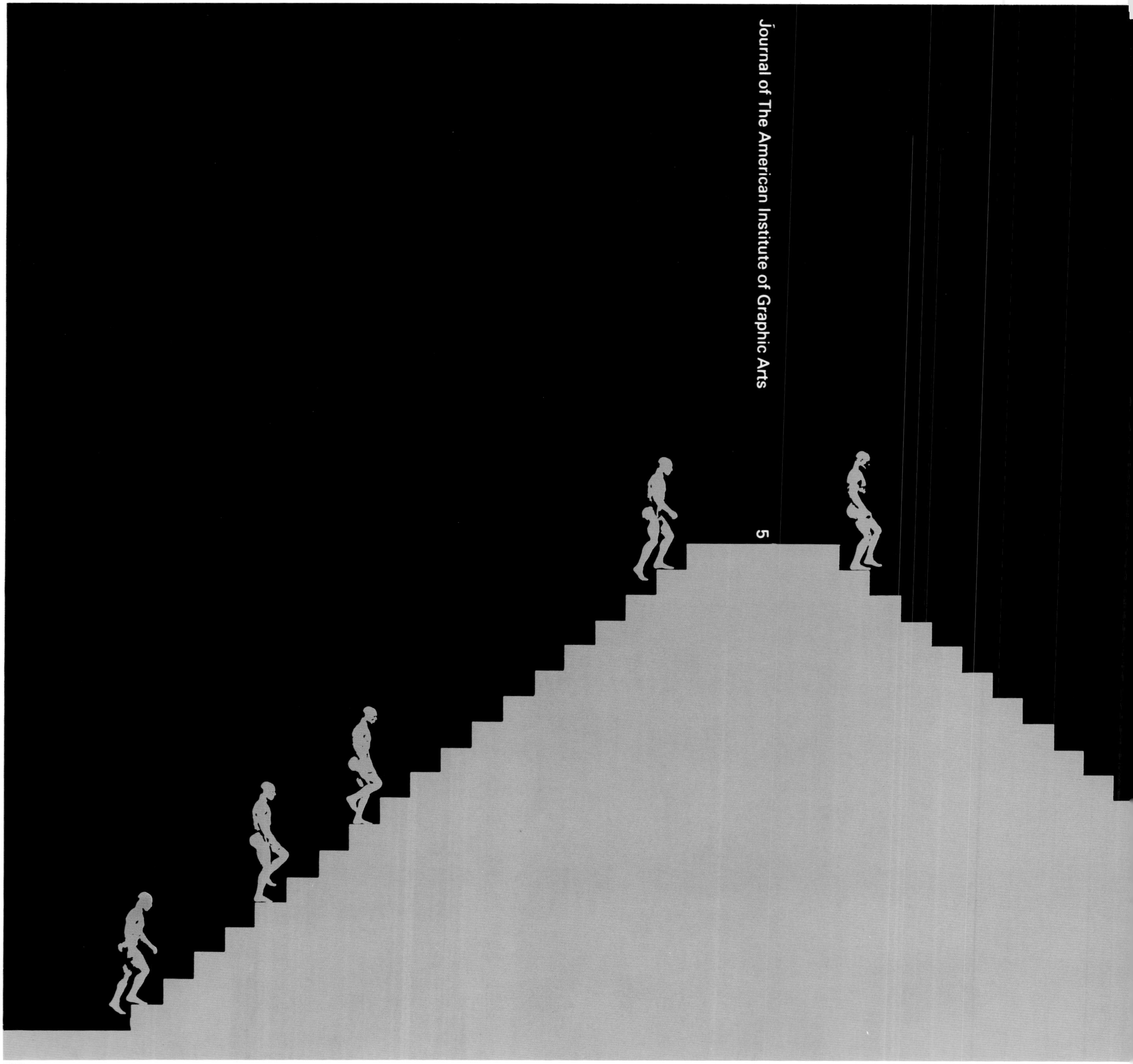

I used that absolutely invaluable reference source, Muybridge's *The Human Figure in Motion*, for the figure. The ziggurat or staircase form recurs in my work.

151

(157, 158)
More staircase variations executed for a Japanese graphic arts magazine. Curiously, as soon as Japanese words appear on a design, the total design for Westerners takes on a Japanese flavor.

現代の代表的イラストレーター

MILTON GLASER ミルトン・グレイサー

アイデア 別冊 誠文堂新光社

昭和43年6月20日発行

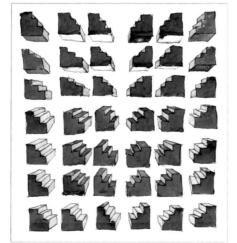

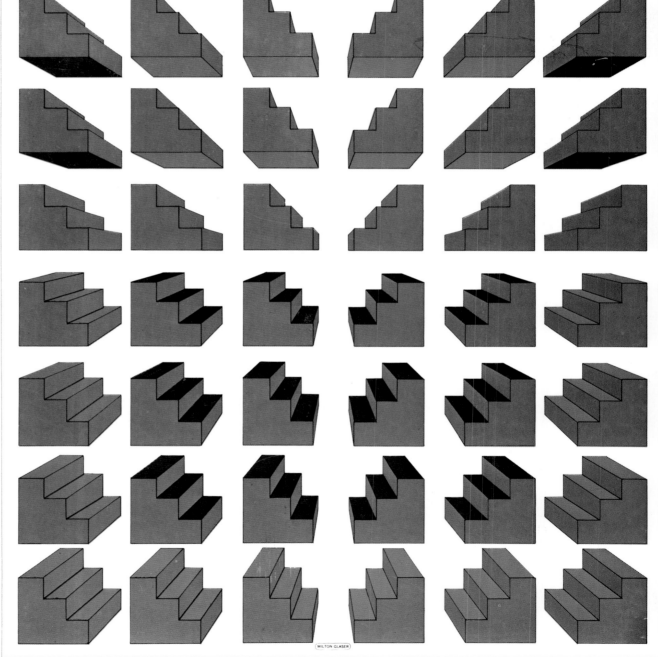

MILTON GLASER

GARBO
AND THE
NIGHT WATCHMEN

EDITED BY ALISTAIR COOKE

(159)
For this dust jacket I combined the staircase with an interesting photomontage made of Garbo during the Thirties. The letterforms may not be sufficiently developed.

This is the first alphabet I
ever designed. For some
inexplicable reason I called
it Babyfat. Because I'm not a
type designer, most of my
alphabets are actually novel-
ties or graphic ideas ex-
pressed typographically. Here
the idea was to take a gothic
letter and view it simultaneously from two sides. It
started out as a rather esoteric
letterform; it ended up being
used in supermarkets for
''Sale'' signs.

154

(162, 163)
The original sketch (162) and
the finished poster (163) for
a concert by Simon &
Garfunkel, the well-known
composer-singers. The letterforms of Babyfat shown on
the previous page (161) led
to the illustrative representation of the performers; usually
the sequence is the reverse.

162

163

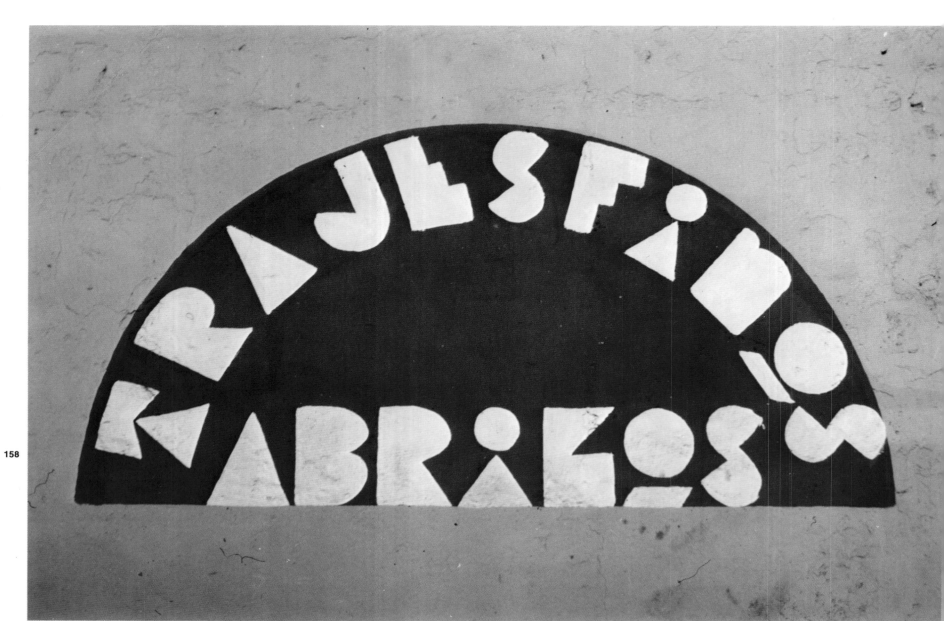

164

(164, 165)
The inspiration for my Babyteeth type face came from this
sign I photographed in
Mexico City (164). It's an
advertisement for a tailor. The
E was drawn as only some-
one unfamiliar with the alphabet could have conceived.
Yet it is completely legible.
I tried to invent the rest of the
alphabet consistent with this
model. At the right (165), a
number of variations on the
Babyteeth theme.

(166, 167)
Hugh Masekela is an African jazz trumpet player. I used African design themes in his costume to establish a background. I also used a variation of my type face called Babyteeth Baroque. The graphic subtlety in this solution emerges from the fact that the shape of Masekela's smile and the openings in the letterform relate.

160

166

G. Keys & Del Shields Present

HUGH MASEKELA

PHILHARMONIC HALL
LINCOLN CENTER

FRIDAY, MAY 12, 8:30 PM

Tickets Available at Box Office Lincoln Center and Bloomingdales TR 4-2424 4.50 4.00 3.50 3.00 2.50

NEO
FUTURA

ABCDE

ABCDE

163

69

ABCDE

(168, 169)
I designed this type face in
three different weights for
greater flexibility. As I mentioned earlier (124), it is
based on Futura.

RESPONSEABILITY

(170, 172)
This spread shows three
different uses of Neo-Futura.
The logo for the first (170)
was developed for The Art
Directors Club Communica-
tions Conference. Word play
suggests that the ability to
respond creates responsi-
bility. This B (171) in a variety
of colors was used as a trademark for Beylarian Limited,
a furniture manufacturer and
importer. The Performance
logo (172) was developed for
the 1973 Aspen Design Conference; the idea behind it
was a search for form within
performance.

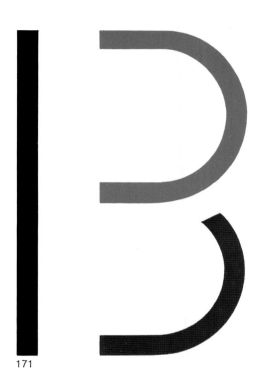

171

PERFORMANCE

172

(173, 174)
This type face is called
Houdini after the famous
American magician. I wanted
to produce a letterform that
would gradually disappear as
one line after another was
removed.

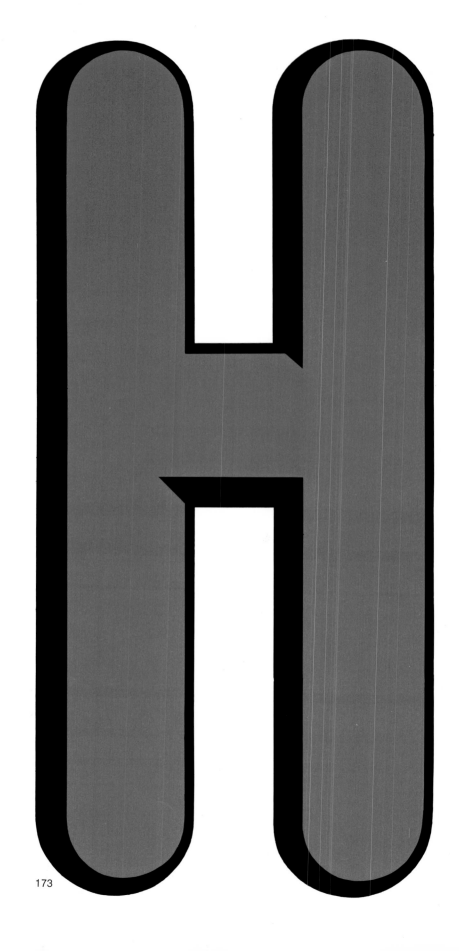

ABCDEFGHIJKLM

ABCDEFGHIJKLM

ABCDEFGHIJKLM

167

ABCDEFGHIJKLM

ABCDEFGHIJKLM

ABCDEFGHIJKLM

(175)
Commissioned by the 1972 Aspen Design Conference, this poster was part of a series that sought to explain urban life. Actually, more a chart than a poster, it is packed with visual and factual information presented in a non-intimidating way. The central idea behind the series was the suggestion of a variety of city phenomena as potential learning experiences.

UNITED ARTISTS/16
IS PROUD TO UNVEIL
A SPECIAL COLLECTION
OF CLASSIC ENTERTAINMENT:
FESTI-FILMS/VOLUME 1
BANANAS
SUNDAY, BLOODY SUNDAY
200 MOTELS
THE DECAMERON
BURN
STREETCAR NAMED DESIRE
THE TOUGH GUYS
FILM FESTIVAL:
PUBLIC ENEMY
LITTLE CAESAR
TREASURE OF THE
SIERRA MADRE
THEY DRIVE BY NIGHT

(176)
Poster announcing a film festival. I had always wanted to develop a cylindrical letter-form and this seemed a good opportunity. The copy reads "Festi-Film is proud to unveil a special collection of classic entertainment," which seemed reason enough to draw a burlesque stripper. As she and the letterforms turn simultaneously, the word "Festi-Films" comes into view.

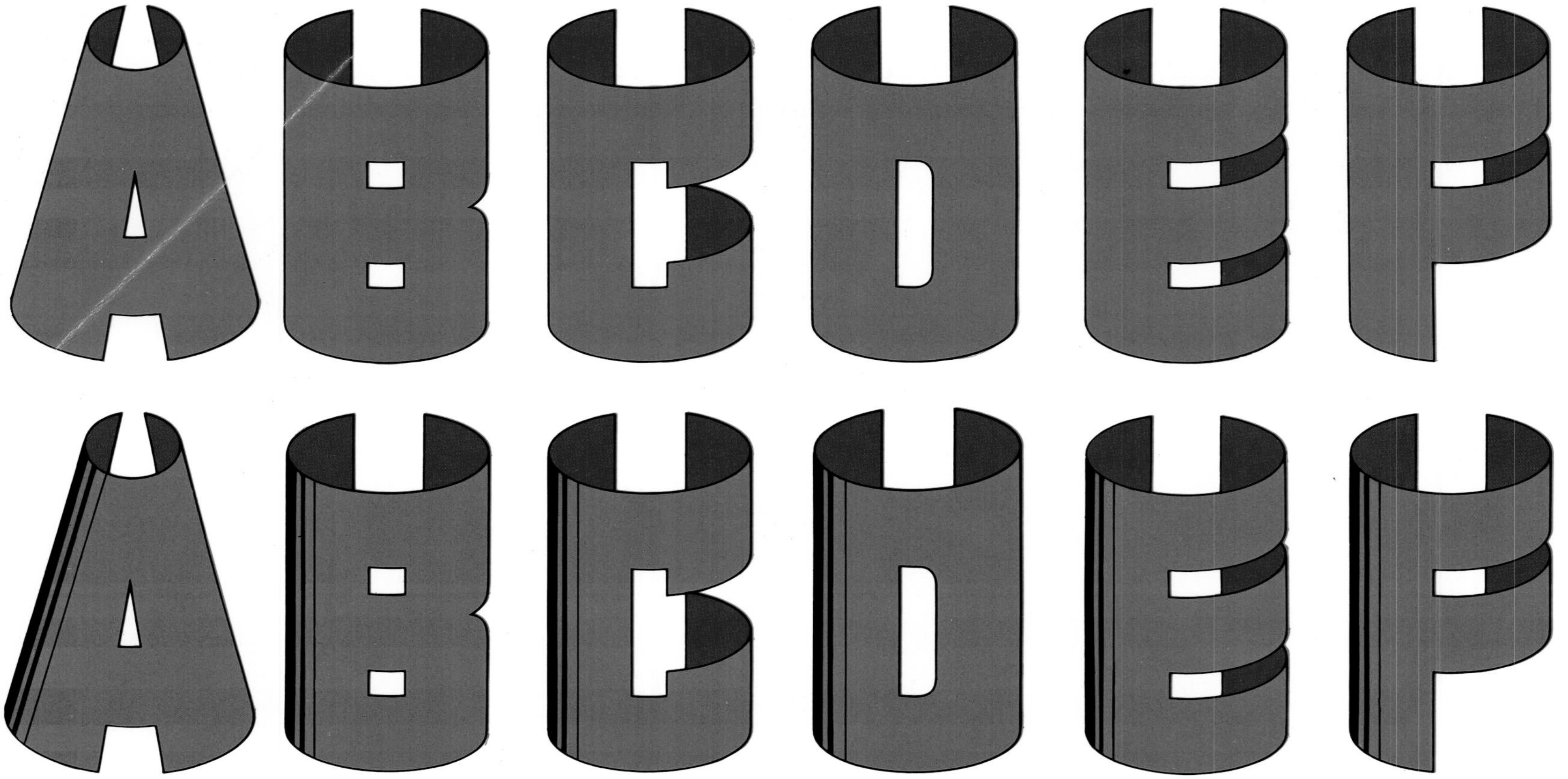

170

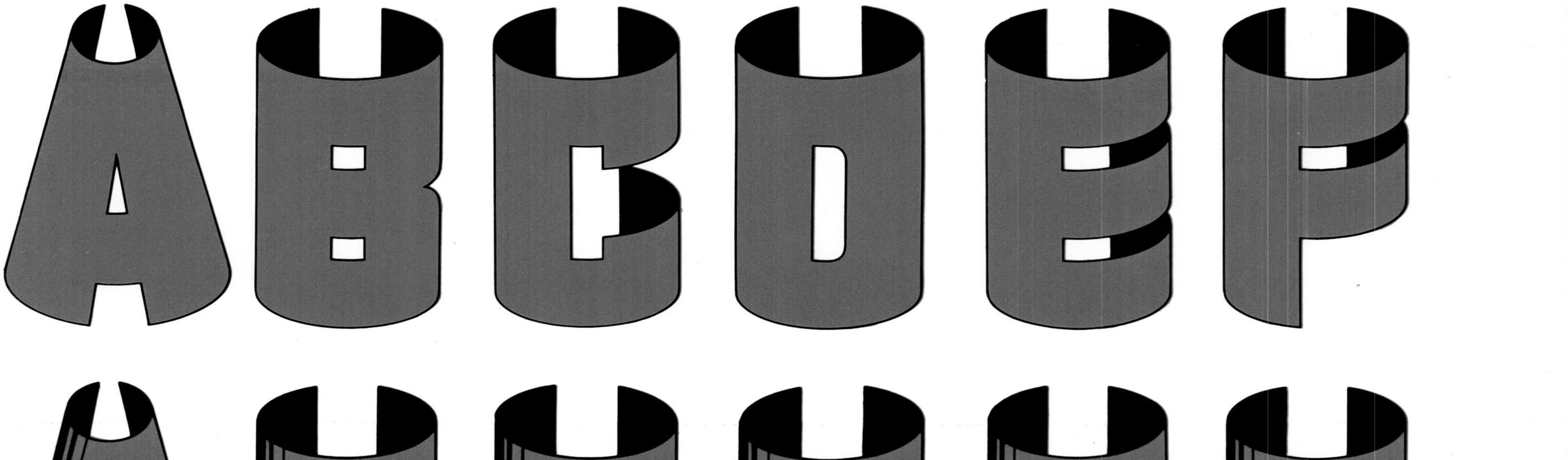

177

The photograph on this page was taken for a poster promoting registration at the School of Visual Arts. It reminds me now of the work of my friend Jean Michel Folon who, in a weak moment, agreed to write the preface to this book.

171

(179)
Asked to design a store for children in New York, in my profound ignorance of what was involved, I said yes.
I went about it in a totally amateurish way, making little paper mock-ups to demonstrate my ideas to the contractors. After considerable confusion, it all worked out. The store is located on 58th Street between Lexington and Third Avenues. There are two doorways, one for adults, the other for children. On opening day one of the company's vice-presidents tried to enter the wrong door and cracked his head on the door frame. The children's door was closed for a year.

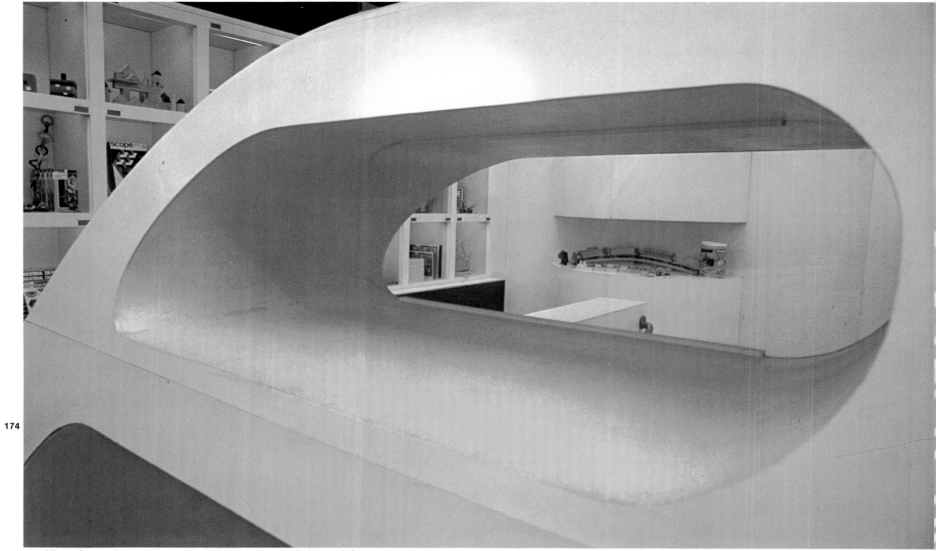

180 View of store through staircase enclosure, display shelves at left.

181 Detail of door handle, logo in metal.

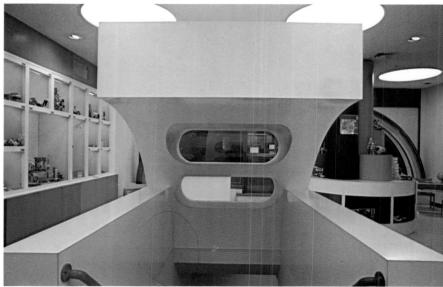

182 Staircase housing, street level.

83 Entrance with little store-posted door signs, contributing to the destruction of the intended effect.

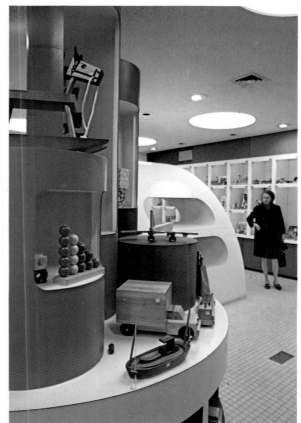

184 General view of the inside.

185 The Childcraft logo.

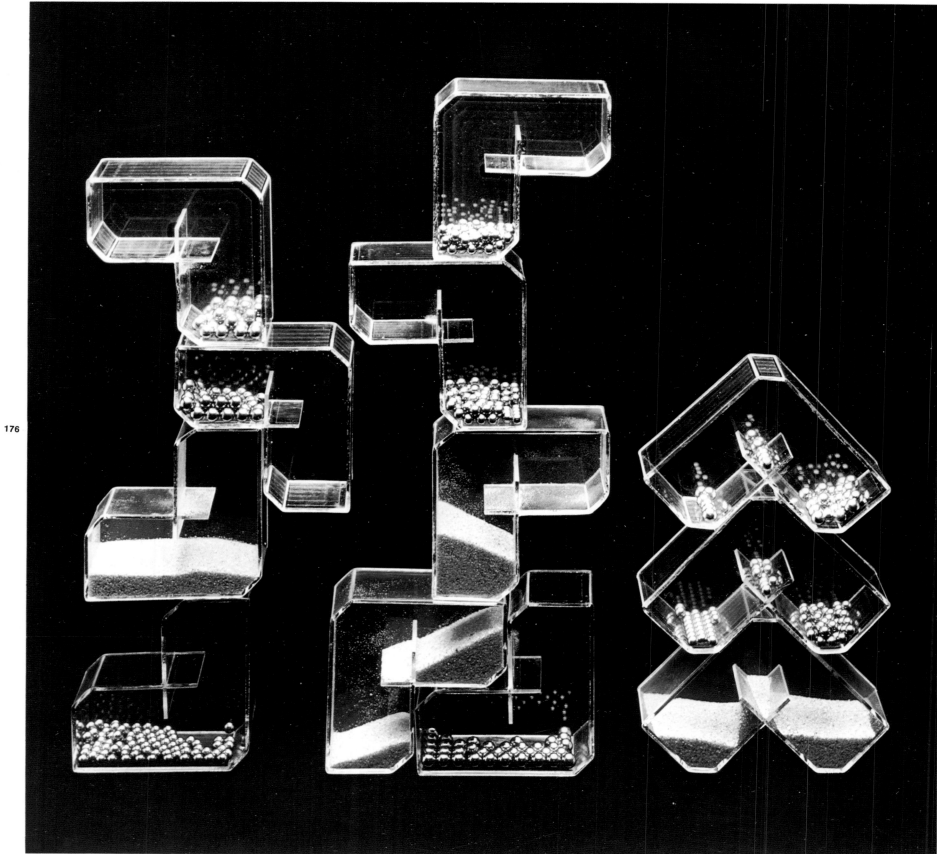

Art in America DECEMBER-JANUARY 1965-66

(186, 187)
These Cubismo blocks on the cover of *Art in America* (187) were commissioned by the magazine as part of a series featuring toys designed by American artists. My idea was to produce a cube made up of sixty-four plastic blocks. Each plane of sixteen blocks contained a different design motif. Most of the blocks were designed so that, placed together, they produced a variety of continuing patterns. The educational premise was to expose the child to the idea of producing a series of changeable images without a naturalistic framework. They sold poorly. Ten years later I was encouraged to try again. For a company called Toys by Artists, I produced L-shaped blocks (186) weighted with either ball bearings or sand. Because of their shape and their shifting weights, the blocks can be arranged in a variety of ways to take advantage of the cantilever effect. From a commercial point of view they have been considerably more successful than the Cubismo blocks.

177

(188)
A School of Visual Arts poster
with two clichés as its basis—
the artist palette and the rainbow. By having the rainbow
pierce the palette an unex-
pected image results. The
subject of the poster was
"career futures in the art
field." This is an example of
how two clichés can be better
than one. More precisely, we
can see here how clichés can
be used to "detoxify" each
other.

178

The Russian T
me to redesign th
mark and menus. I as
could design a vodka dr
as well. My cocktail, called
The Rasputin, consists of a
jigger of vodka, three jiggers
of clam juice, and an anchovy-
stuffed olive. A heady mixture,
it tastes a bit like something
dredged out of the sea and is
surprisingly erotic.

179

…a
…),
ch
…ards
the
…ws. . . .

(192)
Peter the G… …ne first
monarch to invite ladies to
dine at his dinner table. He
demanded that the women of
his court adopt fashionable
hair styles, stop coloring their
teeth black, discard their veils
and appearing in décolleté
gowns. Peter the Great was
fond of Dutch cheeses and
meats served with fruit
preserves.

(193)
Ancient Slavic peoples wor-
shipped the sun and at Spring
solstice cooked his image,
a round cake fried in butter.
As a result the Blini came
into Russian cuisine.

180

190

191

192

193

194

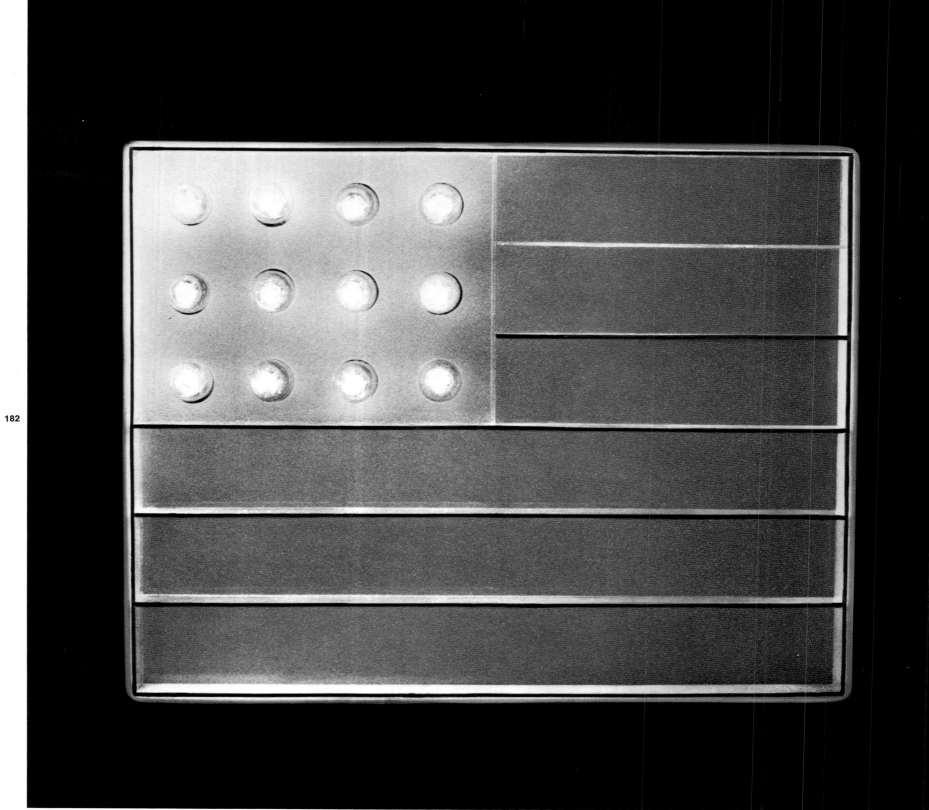

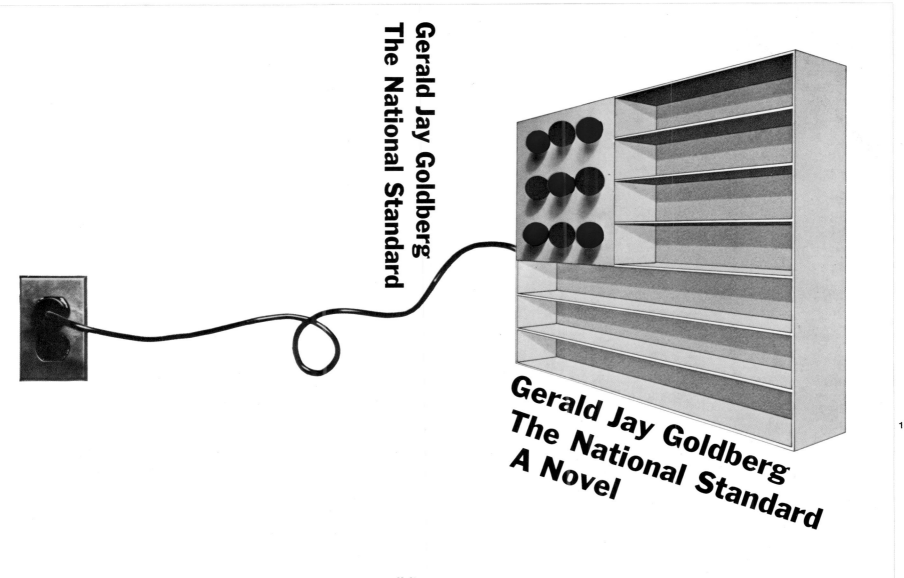

Gerald Jay Goldberg
The National Standard

Gerald Jay Goldberg
The National Standard
A Novel

Holt
Rinehart
Winston

196

(195, 196)
For myself I designed a lamp
based on the American flag.
Two years later I was able to
use it as the motif on a
dust jacket (196).

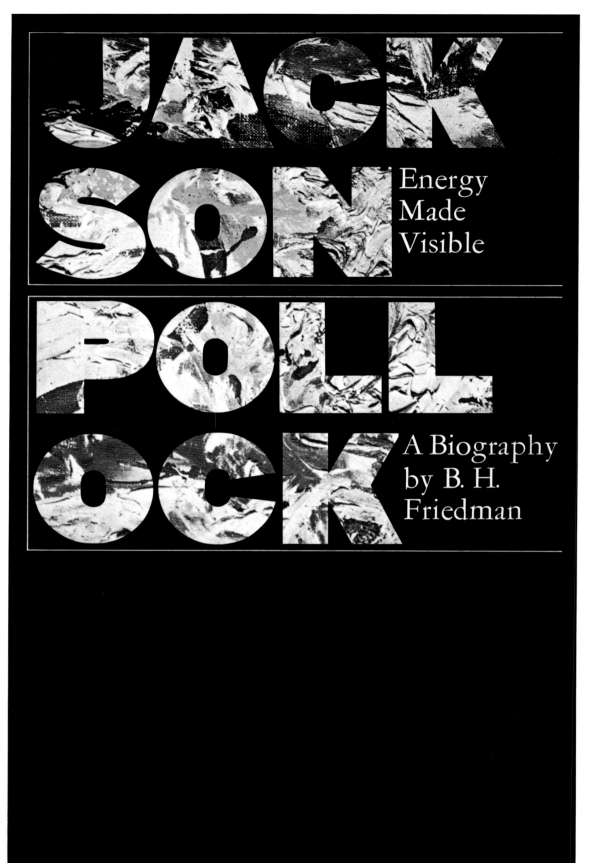

197

198

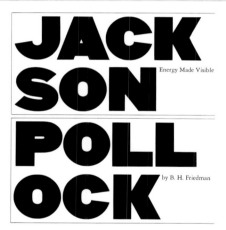

199

Jackson Pollock

J P

Energy Made Visible

During the summer Jackson wrote to Charles:

I haven't much to say about my work and things—only that I have been going through violent changes the past couple of years. God knows what will come out of it all—it's pretty negative stuff so far.... I haven't been up to any of those competitions. Will try when my work clears up a little more. Phil Guston and his wife have been winning some of the smaller jobs. I'm still trying to get back on the project and it doesn't look any too damned good. At best it will be another four or five weeks, and then it may be the army instead.

Jackson got back on the Project in October and during the same month registered for the draft. Sanford wrote to Charles:

They are dropping people like flies on the pretense that they are Reds, for having signed a petition about a year ago to have the C.P. put on the ballot. We remember signing it so we are nervously awaiting the axe. They got 20 in my department in one day last week. There is no redress. The irony of it is that the real Party People I know didn't sign the damn thing and it is suckers like us who are getting it. I could kick myself in the ass for being a damn fool—but who would of thought they could ever pull one as raw as that. Further more, when they get us in the Army with the notion that we are Reds you can bet they will burn our hides. Needless to say we are rigid with fright.

The tensions surrounding the Project and the draft were compounded by Jackson's having to adjust to a new doctor, Violet Staub de Laszlo, another Jungian, to whom Henderson had referred him, having very consciously chosen a woman. Dr. de Laszlo had ideas about the army making a man of Jackson, making him face his responsibilities, and so forth. Despite the history of alcoholism, psychiatric therapy, and brief institutionalization, it was only with great reluctance that she wrote his draft board the letter that, in April, would assure his being classified IV-F.

The previous May, in yet another letter to Charles, Sanford had written: "Jack is doing very good work. After years of trying to work along lines completely unsympathetic to his nature, he has finally dropped the Benton nonsense and is coming out with an honest creative act." Then the good work must have been mainly what he had done while with Dr.

Henderson. But now in July 1941, more than a year later, Sanford would again write to Charles, giving him for the first time detailed information regarding Jackson's psychiatric problems and esthetic progress:

...In the summer of [1938] he was hospitalized for six months in a psychiatric institution. This was done at his own request for help and upon the advice of Doctors and with the help and influence of Helen Marot. For a few months after his release he showed improvement. But it didn't last and we had to get help again. He has been seeing a Doctor more or less steadily ever since. He needs help and is getting it. He is afflicted with a definite neurosis. Whether he comes through to normalcy and self-dependency depends on many subtle factors and some obvious ones. Since part of his trouble (perhaps a large part) lies in his childhood relationships with his Mother in particular and family in general, it would be extremely trying and might be disastrous for him to see her at this time. No one could predict accurately his reaction but there is reason to feel it might be unfavorable. I won't go into details or attempt an analysis of his case for the reason that it is infinitely too complex and though I comprehend it in part I am not equipped to write clearly of the subject. To mention some of the symptoms will give you an idea of the nature of the problem, irresponsibility, depressive mania (Dad), overintensity and alcohol are some of the more obvious ones. Self-destruction, too. On the credit side we have his art which, if he allows it to grow, will, I am convinced, come to great importance. As I have inferred in other letters, he has thrown off the yoke of Benton completely and is doing work which is creative in the most genuine sense of the word. Here again, although I "feel" its meaning and implication, I am not qualified to present it in terms of words. His thinking is, I think, related to that of men like Beckmann, Orozco and Picasso. We are sure that if he is able to hold himself together his work will become of real significance. His painting is abstract, intense, evocative in quality....

Sandy's description of Jackson's latest work suggests his assimilation of the Cubist tradition (particularly the recognition of a flat picture plane) and that of Expressionistic distortion. Though Beckmann's work was not nearly as well known as Picasso's, Pollock would surely have seen it in art publications and probably also at Curt Valentin's Bucholz Gallery and at the Museum of Modern Art. As with Picasso, Pollock would have been moved by Beckmann's intensely personal response to public events.

Contents

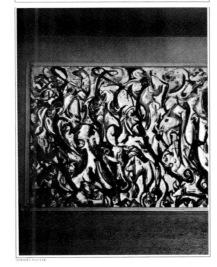

Pollock in front of the approximately eight by twenty-foot mural commissioned in 1943 by Peggy Guggenheim for the hallway of her home and shown—as in this photograph by Pollock's friend, the photographer Herbert Matter—at Miss Guggenheim's Art of This Century gallery in February, 1947. Pollock studied the large blank canvas for six months before painting it in a single session. Pollock's gallery

mate Robert Motherwell said this was "probably the catalytic moment in (Pollock's) art....Dancing around the room, he finally found a way of painting that fitted him, and from then on he developed that technique and that scale." Clement Greenberg, Pollock's critical champion, says it convinced him, even more than previous work, of the young painter's greatness.

(197-203)
I like to design books, but because relatively little money is budgeted by publishers for this purpose in the United States, it's generally an uneconomical activity. In most cases, books are assembled "in house" expeditiously. The realities of publishing economics can be a difficult context for a designer. Here I used the device of a three-sided rectangle to unify the design.

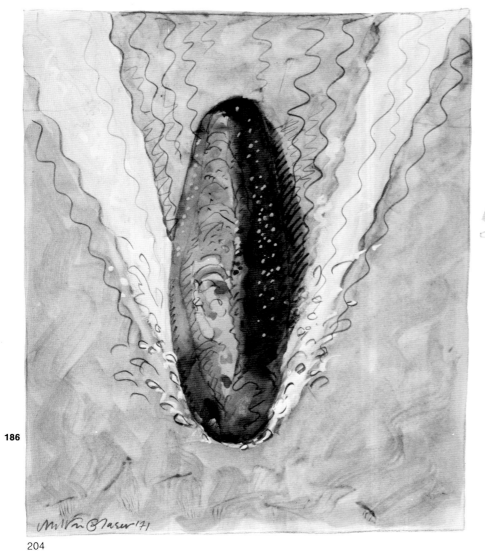

204

205

(204-206)
The sketches (204, 205) here
were preliminary studies for
an exhibition at the American
Institute of Graphic Arts on
the theme of survival. I started
thinking in terms of the basic
elements of survival, particularly images of bread and
water. Then implications of
"casting bread upon the
waters," then the idea of a
raft or a ship made of bread;
from there I moved to the
image of a bread island in the
middle of the sea. I retained
the image of the bread.
I ordered a giant challah, a
Jewish braided bread that
I admired for its sculptural
qualities, and had it nickle-
plated to emphasize its monu-
mentality. I retained the
original baker's label to
restore the symbol's humility.
I can't say any longer what
finally moved me towards this
solution; the image of the
water had long since dis-
appeared, replaced, through
the choice of a particular
bread, by the idea of a survival of a people.

NEW YORK

207

NEW YORK

208

209

210

Using Game Theory to Park Your Car
Badillo's Election Strategy, by Richard Reeves
The Woman Who Spots Best Sellers First

50 CENTS   FEBRUARY 12, 1973

New York

TARGET BLUE

**The Story Behind
The Police
Assassinations
By Robert Daley**

(207-211)
New York first appeared as a tabloid-sized Sunday supplement in *The New York Herald Tribune*. About a year after the newspaper folded, we started a new small-sized weekly slick magazine with the same name, using many of the same features and writers. For some reason, it took us almost two years to understand how to translate the qualities successful in a Sunday supplement into the new format. We discovered—surprisingly enough—that writers are read differently on a smaller page, especially if there is also a change from rough to smooth paper. The writing style had to be more compact and more dramatic. The original supplement—because it never had to sell on newsstands—could run beautiful pictures on its cover with relatively small headlines, while magazine covers must grab potential readers by the lapels since a hundred other magazines clamor for attention. Curiously, the logotype itself represents this change of character. At the top, the old logo (207) based on the Caslon type face: graceful, thin, and elegant. It was redesigned based more on a Bookman type face.(208) This retained the appearance of the old logo, but took on a tougher, bolder, and more aggressive stance. The scotch rule which once enclosed the logo on the old *New York* (209) was fattened up and served as part of the new identification on both the cover and inside pages.

189

190

SPECIAL DOUBLE ISSUE

How to Stay Well and Feel Great in New York
8-Page Pull-Out Guide Rating Manhattan Hospitals

50 CENTS

DECEMBER 18, 1972

NEW YORK

BIG CITY STRESS:
How Much Can You Take?

BREATHE EASY:
You Can Take a Deep Breath

ORTHODONTIA:
How Many Dollars' Worth Do You Need?

DIET:
Eating Ethnic and Staying Thin

EXERCISE:
A Survey Of Places And Methods

PLUS: MANHATTAN'S BEST EMERGENCY ROOMS

(213-215)
In general, the inside style of *New York* is quite straight-forward. A weekly magazine needs a very rigid design system. With tight deadlines and last-minute changes, there is no opportunity for elaborate layout considerations. In addition, the quality of a weekly magazine is to some extent based on presenting news and features in a believable way; the illusion of unmanipulated presentation is the goal. To some extent it is true that the more beautiful a magazine is, the less believable it becomes. In any case, *New York*'s appeal derives from its energy, not its beauty.

VOL. 5 NO. 51

CONTENTS
Special Double Issue: How to Stay Well and Feel Great in New York

DECEMBER 18/25, 1972

The following are registered trade names and the use of these names is strictly prohibited: The Passionate Shopper, The Urban Strategist, The City Politic, Cityscape, and The Global Village. *New York* is published weekly (except for a combined issue the last two weeks in December) by the NYM Corporation, 207 East 32nd St., New York, N.Y. 10016. Copyright © 1972 by the NYM Corporation. All rights reserved. Reproduction without permission is strictly prohibited. Chairman, Milton Glaser; President, Clay S. Felker; Executive Vice-President, Ruth A. Bower; Vice-President, Finance, Anthony M. Carvette. Second-class postage paid at New York, N.Y., and at additional mailing offices. Subscription rates in Continental U.S.: one year, $10; two years, $18; three years, $25. Alaska, Canada, Hawaii, Puerto Rico, Virgin Islands, one year only, $14; elsewhere: one year only, $17. Editorial and Business Offices: (212) 689-3660. Back Issues $1 per copy.
For subscription information write Mr. Joseph O. Oliver, *New York* Magazine, Subscription Department, Box 2979, Boulder, Colorado 80302.
Postmaster: send form 3579 to *New York*, Box 2979, Boulder, Colorado 80302.

New York Advertising Information Service
If there's something advertised in our pages and you want to know about it—from where to buy it to what's on the menu of a restaurant and how much it'll cost, or the rates of a hotel you may read about in *New York*—just call 684-5544 or 684-5545.

Next Issue (January 1): Power in New York City

NEW YORK 3

The Underground Gourmet/Milton Glaser and Jerome Snyder
QUACK MEDICINE

Until two weeks ago "duck soup" meant only one thing to us—the title of the quintessential Marx Brothers film. Then we discovered **Szechuan Cuisine** at 30 East Broadway (corner of Catherine Street, 966-2326), where we learned the true meaning of duck soup.

At the urging of one of the owners, we tried tang kuei duck (the owner called it "Chinese medicine"), a Taiwanese specialty that was brought to the table in an aluminum-foil covered bowl ($2.50). Peeling back the foil, we found a quarter of a duck resting in clear amber-colored broth. The broth was superlative, tasting much like a rich, non-alcoholic burgundy. "Tang-kuei," from which the soup takes its name, is a petrified Szechuan root used for flavoring. It is also believed to have medicinal properties and costs a steep $30 a pound. The duck itself was lean, tender enough to be cut with a spoon, and absolutely delicious.

Despite its name, the restaurant is not limited to Szechuan food. The management takes special pride in its Taiwanese dishes which are similar, in many ways, to the subtle Fukien-style cooking. Several Taiwanese dishes are not yet listed on the menu: squid soup and pork soup (95 cents each—large enough for two); oyster omelet ($1.50), and sautéed squid ($2.25).

Following the current convention, the menu lists the spicy Szechuan dishes in red; the milder items in black. The mild Szechuan Inn soup combines cellophane noodles, Chinese greens and delicate white fishballs in a flavorful broth ($1.50—enough for three). Or there's the spicy shredded pork and Chinese pickled cabbage soup and the hot and pungent soup ($1.30 each).

A section of the menu is devoted to wor bar dishes (variations on the sizzling rice theme) ranging in price from $3 for a spicy hot and sour version to $3.75 for the mixed meat combination. We tried the shrimp wor bar with mushrooms, a good, mild dish served appropriately hissing and sizzling ($3.25).

For the strong of palate, there's fiery, cold hacked chicken in assorted flavors or chicken spiced with pungency ($2.40 each); sliced pork sautéed with fish flavor ($2.50); shredded beef with hot red sauce ($3); whole carp in hot bean sauce ($3.95), and chicken in orange flavor ($3.50).

In addition to the familiar Szechuan dishes, there are several offbeat preparations: snail meat with garlic sauce ($3); fresh crab with Chinese wine sauce ($2.70); fresh clams in lightly spiced sauce ($2.70); cabbage core sautéed with fish flavor ($2.40); omelet with hot garlic sauce ($2.10), and pulverized rice-coated sliced pork, prepared in a steamer ($2.75).

Vegetables are a soothing foil to the more dramatic meat and fish dishes. Particularly good was the cabbage heart with ham, steamed Chinese cabbage in a white, thick sauce accented with pieces of ham ($2).

As is usually the case in Szechuan restaurants, the casserole dishes offer some of the best values. These dishes, which are ample for three or four people, include a casserole with bean cake, sea cucumber, meat ball, noodle, shrimp and snowpeas ($4); assorted meats and vegetables in casserole ($4.25); simmered bean cake with assorted meat ($3.50), and preserved meat casserole ($3.75—requires 24-hour notice).

Szechuan cuisine boasts excellent, inexpensive noodle dishes. One of these, noodles with pork double fried, combines scallions and shredded pork over a nest of crisp stir-fried boiled noodles ($2.10). The noodle dishes are not at all oily here, as they are in many restaurants. A relish of two cabbages, American and Chinese, one unseasoned, the other with a scorching sauce, accompanies all main dishes.

Despite its bright exterior sign, Szechuan Cuisine is easy to miss as it's located on the "wrong side" of the Bowery in Chinatown. The restaurant is sparsely decorated and charmless. But the warmth of the proprietors, Messrs. Dien, Lo and Liu (a chef who doubles at an uptown American restaurant) and their staff, more than makes up for the lack of physical charm. They're offering a special bonus in the evening (except on Saturday and Sunday), a 10 per cent reduction in the price of all dinner checks. Seats 85. Open Monday through Thursday, 11 a.m. to midnight, Friday and Saturday 11 a.m. to 1 a.m., Sunday 11 a.m. to 10:30 p.m. ■

Food—good to excellent
Service—good
Ambience—fair to good
Hygiene—good

NEW YORK 89

New York

Someday We May All Live in Lefrak City

By Andrew Tobias

"...Says one real-estate man of Sam Lefrak: 'He is vulgar, ruthless, egotistical, lacking in warmth, utterly without taste. But the fact remains that he knows his business like nobody else'..."

It's not hard to make fun of a builder who can't pronounce "condominium." But Samuel Jonathan Lefrak, who pronounces his name *Le Frak* (except on social occasions, when it's Le *Frak*) and condominium "condominiun," has housed more New Yorkers in larger apartments at lower rents than any other man in town. He is landlord to a quarter of a million people, mostly middle-income residents of Brooklyn and Queens. A quarter-million more, mostly in Bedford-Stuyvesant, Brownsville, Williamsburg and East New York, live in buildings his father built and sold between the First and Second World Wars. With roughly $10 million in rent rolling in each month, a few million dollars of Texas oil, a few million dollars of big-name art, a few homes with a few in help, a stable of race horses and a "100-foot yacht" that conscience sometimes compels him to admit is only 85 feet long, Sam Lefrak is one of the richest men in the world.

Says he: "A lot of people call me a philanthropist, a civic leader, a community planner, a master builder—I'm an engineer, a 'colonel,' a 'doctor,' I was knighted by Pope John, I wear all kinds of hats—but just call me just plain Sam. I'm a very informal kinduva guy. I guess you get that way when you have a love of people, and that's the way I feel."

Says one real-estate man: "Sam is vulgar, ruthless, egotistical, lacking in any real human warmth, and utterly without taste. But when you get all through detracting from him, the fact remains that in his field he is phenomenal. He knows his business like no-body else." Though many characterize Sam's personal traits less harshly, virtually all agree that he knows his business like nobody else.

The largest individual builder-landlord in the city, if not the country, Sam Lefrak is worth an estimated half-billion dollars. Litton Industries and the Great Atlantic & Pacific Tea Company, based on current market values, are worth nearly as much. Of course, when you are that wealthy, just how wealthy you are is quite a subjective calculation, and Sam prefers to keep his own estimate to himself. Those around him who try to guess the size of his fortune may have more to base their estimates on later this year if Sam goes through with his avowed plan to go public.

Sam has talked of going public for years now, but ultimately has not been willing to relinquish the independence and flexibility of private ownership. Also, he says he doesn't understand the people on Wall Street, and they don't understand him. "They only know how to multiply; they don't know how to add," he says, alluding to his discussions with White, Weld; Merrill Lynch; Loeb, Rhoades, and First Boston. "Look: I could be seduced, but I want to be kissed a little too."

If he finally does go public this year, it will be to aid him in the financing of his latest and most ambitious project, the planned $1.1-billion Battery Park City. The site for Battery Park City is 91 acres in the shadow of the World Trade Center, where Sam envisions "a complete urban microcosm, a city within a city, encircled by a monorail, where a person could be born, live, and die without ever leaving." The Lefrak Organization is managing partner and 50 per cent owner of the venture. Fisher Bros. is the coordinating partner which, with several other firms, owns the other 50 per cent.

Sam says that Battery Park City will comprise 14,100 apartments, 14 per cent of them renting at about $40 a room to low-income tenants (of the senior-citizen rather than the welfare variety, Sam points out), 56 per cent renting at about $80 a room to middle-income tenants, and 30 per cent renting as luxury apartments at about $120 a room. There will be nearly a million square feet of enclosed-mall shopping space, a 1,000-room hotel, underground parking, a marina for large boats, three schools, rooftop ice-skating rinks, a library, a hospital, a fire station, a police station, an esplanade along the river, movie theaters, banks, swimming pools, and Venetian blinds.

Right now the site is virtually barren. Yet Lefrak says construction will begin later this year and that his first tenants will move in an unbelievable fifteen months later. Instead of using bricks, he says, he may prefabricate his building blocks off-site and float them down the Hudson to avoid tying up city traffic, then lift them into place with helicopter sky-cranes. He says he may not paint his apartment walls if he can find the right kind of plastic-coated material. He says he hopes to find a way to use the water of the river in his cooling system, and another way to recycle all the effluent from the project to make it pollution free. He wants to run just one water pipe into each

Sam Lefrak, hard-hatted master builder, on a visit to his South Bronx turnkey unit project at 146th Street and Brook Avenue.

Photographed by Dan Brown

36 NEW YORK

(216-219)
When stories are unrelated to hard news, layout can be more interesting. For one thing, there is more time to design them; for another, they don't need the directness of a news story. This kind of spread functions as relief from the magazine's more consistent rhythm. At top (216) a magazine spread adapting the Chinese grocery store poster. Below (217), a story about growing up in the Bronx with which I identified and wanted to illustrate. At top (218), a spread identifying a variety of pastries from Chinatown. Below (219), a characteristic spread from the Fall catalog issue, somewhat more flamboyant from the design point of view.

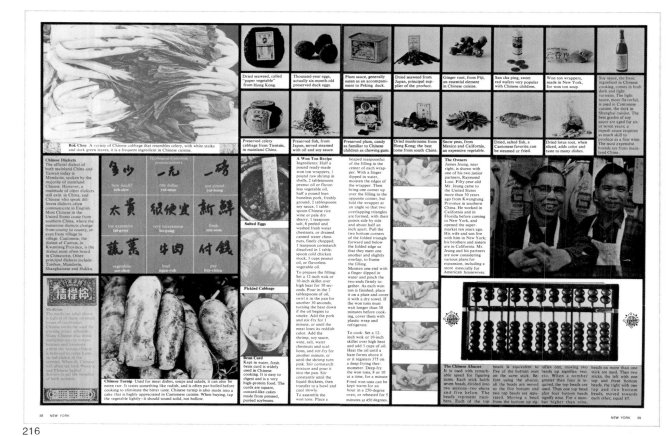

216

217

The Sweet Side of Chinatown

Photographed by Ben Somoroff

As we've noted, some Dim Sum parlors offer special Chinese pastries. Many of these are based on rice flour and so our Western palates are not accustomed to their texture than cake. In any case, you'll find these pastries considerably less sweet than their Western counterparts — some of the strongest and curiously beautiful specialties are readily available.

1. Sweet Ginger Cake (Tim-Woo-To-Ko)
Thick, firm pudding fortified with small pieces of ginger throughout, a meal in itself. Price: 20 cents.

2. Black Sesame Roll
(Hat Fu Mun)
76 Mott St.
Frustrating appearance, sweet mild taste. Chewy rice-flour and sesame roll. Too chewy for walking but hard daily to eat-chat completely, harmless. Price: 25 cents.

3. Coconut Macaroon (Yeh-Sant)
Source: Fung Wong Bakery.
Light golden dome with most cake then brittle sugar crust, very acceptable to Western taste. Price: 20 cents.

4. Sesame Seed Cake (Soo-Joe-Gee)
Source: Long Moon Bakery.
Lantern dome. Pale red outer dome, coated with pieces of colored tough Jello—lackluster taste. Price: 25 cents.

5. Sesame Seed Roll (Soo-Foo)
Source: Wah-San Coffee Shop.
Tough hollow dough where exterior studded with sesame seeds; interior soft with sweet bean paste. Price: 15 cents.

6. Nut Pie (Tin-Yan-Ko)
Source: Fung Wong Bakery,
83 Mulberry St.
Translucent fine-cut gelatin top, marshmallow gum meringue center; spongy alternate. Price: 15 cents.

7. Steamed Cookie (Tai-Chow)
Source: Wah-Loon Coffee House.
Overspongy, crumbly big brother to the almond cookie. Price: 25 cents.

8. Steamed Cookie
(Shung-Kwo-Fan-Fa)
Source: Wah-San Coffee Shop.
Formed bean paste larded through layer. Rigid, flaky outer cone and nuts. Pastry covering. Sweet, pungent alternate. Price: 15 cents.

9. Pink Flake
Source: Wah-San Coffee Shop.
Oversweet of synthetic banana flavor, almond paste texture — sweet and dense. Price: 20 cents.

10. Moon Cake (Yit Pen)
Source: Koon Shing, 202 Canal St.
Paste-like crust, lotus seed or bean paste filling. Price: 70 cents.

11. Sesame Cake (Siew-Han-Ju)
Source: Fung Wong Bakery.
Crumbly cross between a hard doughnut and an oily cupcake.
Price: 35 cents.

12. Rice Cake (Bock Fan-Koh)
Source: Wah-San Coffee Shop.
Translucent white moist rice flour —chewy texture, slightly fermented sweet taste. Price: 15 cents.

13. Pink Flake
(Shung-Kwo-Fan-Fa)
Source: Wah-San Coffee Shop.
Shocking pink, flaky, heavy pastry covering a Chinese date-fruit cake with the embedded hard-cooked egg yolk. Price: 65 cents.

14. Doughnut (Joc-Lam-Nye)
9 Doyers St.
Sunshine but oily, terrible cruller.
Price: 20 cents.

15. Dinner Roll (Mon Bau)
Source: Fung Wong Bakery.
An egg-enhanced bread that looks and tastes like a sweetened Jewish challah. Price: 20 cents.

16. Chinese Egg Custard Doughnut (Egg Custard Garden)
Source: Lai-Gong Coffee Garden.
Thin crust, flaky doughnut outside — cloudy packed egg custard inside. Price: 20 cents.

17. Fried Rice Cake (Koh-Mar)
Source: King's Coffee and Tea House, 9 Elizabeth St.
Sticky, sugary, sweet, oily amalgam of rice, noodle, sesame seed and bean paste. Price: 20 cents.

18. Red Bean Paste Cake
(Loo-Co)
Source: Lai-Gong Coffee &
Tea Garden, 65 Bayard St.
Alternate layers of opaque gray gelatinous rice flour with red sweet red bean paste. Price: 20 cents.

19. Chinese Cake (Soo-Bo)
Source: Fung Wong Bakery,
30 Mott St.
Chinese muffin filled with sweet plum paste, chewy but not bad. Better warm. Price: 20 cents.

20. Meat-Flavored Dumpling
(Ka-Tan-Ko)
Source: Koon Shing, 202 Canal St.
Compacted, silvery cake-like pastry lotus seed paste filling like chocolate. Price: 20 cents.

21. Lotus Seed (Lin Young)
Source: Koon Shing, 202 Canal St.
Hard and compacted dome made with mashed-potato-like filling and small fragment of seed. Price: 20 cents.

22. Steamed Sponge Cake
(Kai-Tan-Ko)
Source: Fung Wong Bakery.
More like a sponge than cake — slightly sweet. Price: 20 cents.

Theater

THE SUNSHINE BOYS

Simon's "Sunshine."

This is the Neil Simon comedy without which the Broadway season would hardly be complete. His twelfth script in twelve years brings together Jack Albertson and Sam Levene as a vaudeville team that hasn't spoken in ten years (a very odd couple) but is called to give one last turn on a TV comedy special. Alan Arkin is the director. Opening at the Broadhurst December 20.

DEAR OSCAR

Wilde set to music by Caryl Young and Addy O. Fieger, with the musical staging of Donald Saddler. Opening at the Broadway Theater November 12.

Oscar Wilde

WE BOMBED IN NEW HAVEN

Since Joseph Heller's play got high marks in a student production at Storm King High School earlier this year, it is being revived off-Broadway with at least one Storm King student, Gary Springer, in the cast. Opening at Circle in the Square (downtown) September 24.

VIA GALACTICA

As the first space-age musical, with the second Galt MacDermot score of the season, Via has an interplanetary plot line in which Raul Julia as a spaceship captain visits his girl Virginia Vestoff on the asteroid Ithaca. Spatial illusions are created by scenery projected on a head-on cyclorama, a spaceship that really gets airborne, and a stage floor that behaves like a trampoline. Directed by England's Peter Hall, the show opens the 1,850-seat Uris Theater, first of Broadway's big office-building theaters, on November 21.

Cosmic Chorus in "Via Galactica."

6 RMS RIV VU

Bob Randall's comedy comes out of the classified pages; Jerry Orbach and Jane Alexander, converging on an empty apartment with a view of the Hudson, meet without their spouses and decide to spend a while together. Opening at the Helen Hayes October 17.

THE SCHOOL FOR SCANDAL

"The School for Scandal."

This will be the first in a series by the City Center Acting Company, formerly Juilliard Acting Company, under the over-all supervision of John Houseman, one of the theater's national resources (September 28). Later: **U.S.A.** in the Paul Shyre version (October 1), **The Hostage** (October 10), **Next Time I'll Sing to You** (October 15), **Women Beware Women** (October 17), and **The Lower Depths** (October 24), all at the Good Shepherd-Faith Church next door to Juilliard.

BUTLEY

Last season's London hit by Simon Gray will bring Alan Bates to Broadway as the untidy university professor who returns on a miserable Monday after a barren weekend to his unread exam papers. He has lost his wife to one cold lover, lost his roommate to another young man, and repeatedly dismisses eager tutorial students. As an all-time loser, Bates gives a tour de force performance. Not to be missed. Opening at the Morosco October 31.

Bates as Butley

PHOENIX

In a new incarnation, T. Edward Hambleton's Phoenix Theater reopens in December at its old stand, the Lyceum Theater, with a two-play repertory consisting of O'Neill's **The Great God Brown**, directed by the musical theater's Hal Prince (December 10), and Molière's **Don Juan**, directed by Stephen Porter (December 11). Preceding and following the New York engagement will be a tour by the seventeen-member company headed by John McMartin and Paul Hecht.

PIPPIN

An original musical idea by composer-lyricist Stephen Schwartz (*Godspell*) deals with Charlemagne's son as he embraces a variety of different lifestyles. With a book by Roger O. Hirson, which starts off the story as a magic show, *Pippin* is being brought to the stage by a top professional team—Bob Fosse as director-choreographer; Tony Walton, sets; Patricia Zipprodt, costumes; Jules Fisher, lights; Stuart Ostrow, producer. Eric Berry plays Charlemagne, John Rubinstein his son. Opening at the Imperial October 23.

Theater

Michael Cacoyannis's "Lysistrata"

LYSISTRATA

Melina Mercouri, the Grecian Dietrich, comes to us in a new version by Michael Cacoyannis with music by Peter Link (*Salvation* and *Much Ado About Nothing*), reinterpreted in the light of new wars and women's lib. It will open at the Brooks Atkinson Theater (which has been fitted with orchestra-surrounding ramps for the occasion) on October 24.

THE AMBASSADORS

The first musicalization of a Henry James novel, *The Ambassadors* will star Howard Keel and Danielle Darrieux (they played the roles together last season in London). Music by Don Gohman, lyrics by Hal Hackady, book by Don Ettlinger. To be directed by Stone Widney, an associate of Alan Jay Lerner. Opening at the Lunt-Fontanne November 18.

COMEDY

A musical for fourteen comedians based on *The Great Magician*, with a book by Lawrence Carra, who is also the director (and was the director of the early off-Broadway musical hit, *Leave It to Jane*, in 1959). Tentatively cast: Diane Findlay, George S. Irving, Joe Bova, and Bill McCutchen. It will open either November 26 or December 26. Theatre to be selected.

THE LINCOLN MASK

Vincent J. Longhi reveals some of the lesser-known faces of Lincoln with television's Fred Gwynne as Lincoln and Eva Marie Saint as Mary Todd Lincoln, directed by Gene Frankel and opening at the Plymouth on October 15. Later, a second Lincoln play, **The Last of Mrs. Lincoln**, by James Pirdeaux, with Julie Harris, will open at ANTA on November 26.

Fred Gwynne as Lincoln

TRICKS

Originated by Jon Jory at the Actors Theater of Louisville, *Tricks* is a lively musical version of Molière's fast-moving *Les Fourberies de Scapin* which Herman Levin, of *My Fair Lady*, is bringing to Broadway, at a theater to be selected, in mid-December. The rock score is by Jerry Blatt, lyrics by Lonnie Burstein. Also: finger puppets, hand puppets, sliding panels, trap doors, gymnastics.

Colleen Dewhurst

MOURNING BECOMES ELECTRA

Circle in the Square opens a second house, designed in the same three-sided proportions as its old, but twice as big, in the new Uris Building on Broadway. O'Neill's epic drama will star Colleen Dewhurst and Janice Rule. Michael A. Shultz will direct the three-and-a-half-hour production as the first of three plays for the uptown Circle season. Opening November 2. ■

(220, 221)

Audience was a completely different design problem. As a hardcover periodical, it came out every two months and was sold only by subscription. It's target audience was people interested in art, photography, poetry, and good fiction. The publisher and editor were delightful and the magazine was completely designed and illustrated at the Studio. The printing was beautiful. In short, a designers dream! A cross between a magazine and a book, *Audience* carried no advertising, which made it possible to design it with no unplanned visual interruptions. Survival without advertising is difficult and *Audience* died bravely in its third year. Since it didn't compete on the newsstands, *Audience* covers could be abstract or even obscure, as long as they were interesting. There was the additional blessing of not having to deal with four or five headlines.

194

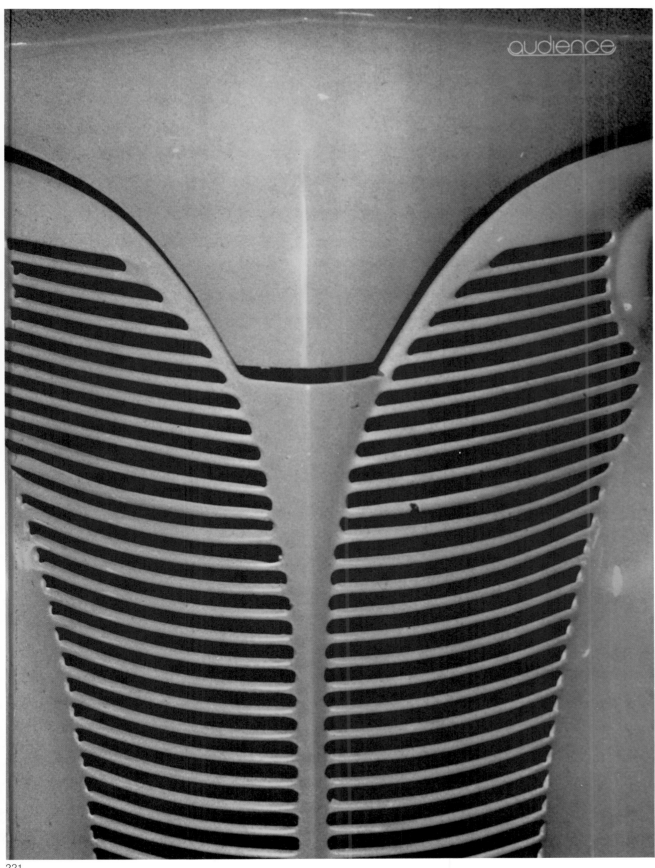

(222)
The design of *Audience* was a cooperative venture involving Seymour Chwast, Vincent Ceci, and myself. This cover was drawn by the fine American illustrator, Barbara Nessim.

Notes from Inner Space

Three Caves in Southern Missouri by C. W. Gusewelle.

They have come on a brittle winter afternoon — Roy and Jeannette with their frozen smiles — to see if this time they might make a union that no man will put asunder. Have come to the very place where Prince Buffalo, a Big Hills Osage, took to wife and may even have bedded sweet Irona who was of the Little Hills faction.

Buffalo and his Irona have gone to dust, but the greatness of their love lives on under the careful stewardship of Eddie Miller, the manager of Bridal Cave. In the twenty-three years since the cave was opened to the public, five hundred sixty-six couples have said their vows there. The pictures of some of them are displayed on the walls of the souvenir shop on the bluff above the cave entrance.

"You'll be the five-hundred-sixty-seventh," Eddie Miller tells Jeannette and Roy. "It's a world record." And though his grin is fixed, the groom's eyes go bugging in absolute wonderment from face to face and finally to the shelves of gewgaws, looking anywhere to discover *Why me?*

"Yeah, but how many of them's still married?" one of the men, husband of Roy's niece, asks Eddie Miller.

"Listen here," Jeannette says, "if he thinks he's gonna divorce me he's outa his head."

The bride's father is wandering among the shelves.

"Hey, c'mere," he calls. "Lookit here." He is holding a box with a cellophane window and three corncobs inside. Two reds and a white.

In an Emergency, it says, *Break Glass. Directions: Use red cob first. Then use white cob to see if you need other red cob.*

"Gimme a dollar and I'll sing for you," Roy's nephew-in-law tells him.

The bugging eyes fix on him. "I'll give y' five dollars *not* to sing."

Eddie Miller is watching through the window.

"I guess the preacher hasn't forgot," he says, and the bride's face gets a sudden no-funny-business look. But Eddie meant it for a joke. "He'll be along pretty soon."

A car pulls into the gravel parking area, bearing customers — a boy in buckskin and a girl in saucer-sized pink sunglasses. They come into the heated building and give Eddie their dollar seventy-five apiece.

"When's the tour start?" the boy asks.

"Right after these folks get married," Eddie tells him. "You might as well see the wedding and start from there."

"Crazy," the boy says. He looks at his girl.

"Crazy," she agrees.

ILLUSTRATED BY MILTON GLASER.

1951 ANGLIA BY DANIELS & CURRY

1939 FORD BY GUY SPOONLEY

(223, 224)
On these three pages are other examples of the range and variety of layout and art styles that *Audience* employed.
For an article about animals living in total darkness, I punched a series of pinholes in a sheet of black paper and lit them from behind with colored lights. They were then photographed and reproduced (221) in color. (222) Photographic details for an editorial portfolio of a hotrod painting exhibition.

(225-228)
Because *Audience* had a
special kind of reader, we had
greater freedom illustrating
it than would have been
possible with a more broadly
based public. In illustrating
stories, I always seek a solution parallel to the text rather
than a repetition of it, so the
text illuminates the picture
and vice versa. We used a
remarkable series of Steve
Salimeri photographs (225) of
people in their bedrooms for a
story about New York's urban
complexities. Below, (226)
we attempted to contrast the
quality of old engravings with
recent photographs of similar
subjects. The story concerned
the metamorphosis of novels
into films on the opposite page
(227) a variety of different type
faces express the quality of
different voices engaged in
conversation. Finally, (228) old
medicine containers were used
to illustrate a story about an
old age home.

225

226

suppose they still do.

WS I remember you read a couple of short stories to us one night. I think short stories make the perfect readable commodity – a manageable length, and one does not drone on too long.

A **Willie Morris told us that you have a short story about your grandfather arriving in this country?**

AM Yeah, my father.

A **He says it is absolutely marvelous and that we must move heaven and hell to get you to let us have it.**

AM Well, it was part of something else, that's why I didn't let it go. I wanted to do more with it, and I haven't had time.

A **Is it related to the play? It seemed to me that Morris told Geoff Ward that it was related to the play, the one you're working on.**

AM Well, in a way it is. But only remotely. That wasn't the reason that I — I thought I would write a large kind of memoir, which I started to do, then stopped doing. I haven't decided quite what form to do it in. It's not quite ready. Willie read sort of the raw material, which is — it could be published.

A **Lord knows, we'd love to do it. Is it true you sometimes write a short prose version of what later becomes a play?**

AM Well, that happens. But I generally don't publish them, because it gets broken off somewhere, and suddenly I realize I'm writing a precis of what I feel I can do better on the stage. It seems to me that there are a lot of words on the prose page (*laughs*) and sometimes with five exchanges of dialogue it seems to me I make it come to life, you know. Whereas on the printed page it doesn't quite do that.

A ***(to Styron)* You can't agree with that.**

AM No, no, I mean for me. I'm looking for an audience, I suppose.

A **You're imagining an audience.**

AM Yeah, yeah.

WS Well, I've noticed just recently in writing this movie script I've been working on with John Marquand – it's my first attempt since college to do something in dramatic form – it's not for the stage, it's strictly for film. But I feel the enormous sense of immediacy and aliveness...

AM *Isn't* it!?

WS It's such a sense of freedom to be unshackled from the restraints of those formal, stately, Latinate...

AM It's vulgar! It's vulgar!

WS (*laughs*) Yes, but...

AM I mean vulgar in the *old* sense, it belongs to the people.

WS Yeah, yeah, you're *talking* here. These lines are just rolling out from your characters, and they have such a sense of freshness, even when possibly they're not very good. Nevertheless, you're not sitting down with that ghastly moment, the famous moment Paul Valéry describes, when he says he *could not write that line*. That's why he never wrote a novel. The line being – what is it? – "the duchess went out at five in the afternoon –" I mean, that is the bane and horror of being a prose writer. The furniture. Moving people in and out of rooms.

AM (*laughs*) To me, there's a screen — I love prose, I love to write it and read it — it is a different screen, though, between yourself and the reader or the audience. And I always feel the screen is down — in other words, that dialogue is evidence. It's a delusion, of course, because after all you're creating the dialogue too. I mean, if a man comes to the door, you can describe him, but suddenly he says something, and it all changes. *He is a witness to himself*. And you're standing aside and not there.

A **But aren't you just giving over the aspects of delineation or description to the actor for appearance, and to the set-designer for the room?**

AM Excepting you're in great control. You could argue that you're in as much control as you are on the printed page, because how many misinterpretations — (*to Styron*) as you can be the witness — can there be to a novel. I mean, the reader's left to his own devices. And he hasn't *got* the control you could exercise over his imagination by selecting the actor, and by inflecting the lines. The controls are there. The problem is that most playwrights vacate because they're overwhelmed by the professionalism of other collaborators, like the director and the actors, and they simply walk away from the whole business. But you don't have to necessarily.

WS That's I think the strength and the weakness of drama, of the *task* of playwrighting, if I get it correctly. The weakness being, okay, you've written a masterpiece, but a masterpiece can be destroyed by a horrible performance. Whereas a work of prose – fiction, let us say – doesn't yield itself to that kind of destruction. You have a bad reader, but that's the reader's fault. The work itself –

AM Stands there.

WS – has its own integrity.

A ***(to Styron)* You had a lot of bad readers with *Nat Turner*, didn't you?**

WS Well – it's complicated. *(laughs)* Yes, I guess I had a lot of bad readers.

A **Did you ever do that piece called "Nobody Knows De Trouble I Seen" about it?**

WS Well, someday I'm either going to do it myself, or – a lot of people have said they wanted to do it and have asked if I have the information. I have a bushel basket full of stuff that I would love to give to somebody I trust someday to put together in a way that would put it all in perspective. There's probably been more controversy on *Nat Turner* than any American novel since Harriet Beecher Stowe's. In fact, there are now two books out on the controversy itself. But what they are, are merely collections of essays that have been written about the book.

A **Yes. *(to Miller)* Have *you* ever had a missed reaction? Did *The Crucible* have any of that kind of . . .**

AM Oh, sure. So did *Salesman* to a degree, but that's all been forgotten. But *The Crucible* was certainly completely dismissed by a large part of the people — and in anger, too. Because it was regarded as a specious defense of the Communists, namely that: there were no witches, but there *are* Communists.

WS Uh huh, I remember that.

AM A lot of angry stuff came out of that.

A **Did you answer at the time, the way Bill is considering an answer?**

AM Yeah, I did. I had some interviews and tried to answer it. But of course at that time the furies were riding high. In the McCarthy times the winds were blowing so fast you couldn't hear yourself think. And I don't recall any important person coming to the defense of even the principle involved, let alone the play itself.

WS You mean, when you say that, there was for instance no long responsive essay in the Sunday *Times*, saying: let's put this matter straight.

AM No, there wasn't. They would have just as soon forgot the whole thing. It took about four to five years before the play was done again, off-Broadway.

WS Then it damaged the play at the time?

AM Oh, definitely, definitely. You see, I'd just had *Death of a Salesman* on, which was an immense hit. And this play came in, and it wasn't all that long later. As soon as the sense of what it was about became apparent, you could feel a coating of ice over that audience. It was just thick enough to *skate* on. It was sheer *terror*. It was *real* terror. I had been in the theater a long time by that time and I'd never experienced such a sensation. In fact, people I knew quite well — newspaper people and so on — when I was standing in the back of the theater and they came out, didn't turn to nod to me.

A ***(whispers)* Wow!**

AM It was as though I — It was at the Martin Beck Theater, I'll never forget that evening — and, you know, newspaper columnists and people I didn't know all that well, but I *knew* them, they'd interviewed me, and we'd shaken hands a few times. And they walked right past me as if I was another post holding up the ceiling. It was quite something.

WS Yes. Well, that must have been at least as unsettling to you as it was to me when I had my reaction, because yours was coming not from a minority group as mine was, although – alas! – it was coming from the minority I had written about. Nonetheless, the hostility *you're* describing was coming from your peers, so to speak.

AM It came from almost every quarter. And it was frightening to me because at that time no one

dered too why no one else was out here in the plaza taking the sun. It was so warm today, almost like summer.

Checking his watch again, he found it was now four-sixteen, and when he looked back at the parking lot there was his mother, fifty yards away, waving to him from the seat of a bizarre little electric vehicle that looked more than anything else like an overdramatized golf cart. It was painted a dazzling, bilious yellow and ran toward him silently at about five miles an hour on three fat pneumatic tires decorated with pink sidewalls. Stretched overhead, like a surrey bonnet, was a yellow- and pink-striped canopy complete with a fringe of gaily jerking tassels. His mother, piloting the cart with a sort of joy stick, glided smartly up to the edge of the plaza and swung to a neat stop.

"Hi! Hop aboard!" she called.

"Say, this is quite a contraption," Emmet replied, leaning in under the canopy to kiss her. "Hello, Mother. You're looking well. Isn't that a new hat?"

"Fairly. Like it?" It was a wide, flatly conical straw, bright lavender in color with red and orange cutout felt blossoms sewn all around. In its garishness, Emmet thought it made his mother's face look older and more deeply lined than ever; her white skin vaguely transparent.

"Yes, very nice," he lied. "And new slacks too. My goodness, aren't we getting to be the sporty young lady."

"Well, come on," his mother said, pleased. "Hop in and we'll spin you straight up to the house."

"Wouldn't miss it," Emmet smiled, scrunching awkwardly in under the canopy. "How long have you had this hot rod, anyway?"

"Isn't it marvelous?"

"Sure is." The top wasn't quite tall enough for his head nor the forward well deep enough for his legs, and he found himself wedged bolt upright with his neck hooked forward and his knees canted awry like some grotesque, captive bird crated for shipment to a zoo. "Well, fine," he said, inching his head around toward his mother, moving carefully so as to avoid her seeing his discomfort. "This must be very convenient for you. Zipping all over the place. Fun too, I'll bet." But the fact that she fit so neatly into the cart somehow troubled him. It made her seem suddenly shrunken and hapless, a tiny nonsense creature doomed to scoot through her few remaining days in a silly electric go-cart and an even sillier hat. Not the mother he knew at all. "How's Dad feeling," he asked, wanting something else to think about.

"Unfortunately," his mother said, angling the cart away from the plaza and back into

the parking lot. "Well, frankly, he's just become awfully difficult since this hip business. Just very demanding and difficult."

"I'm sorry to..." He saw instantly the mistake he had made.

"He demands almost constant attention. Just won't leave me alone for five seconds."

"I..."

"Badgering and pestering. Calling for things every other second. Complaining about the bedclothes. Complaining about the meals I fix him. Won't take his medicine."

"I know."

"I try. Lord knows that. I do every single thing I can think of to make him comfortable..."

"Maybe..."

"Sometimes I just want to sit down and cry."

"Oh, well..."

"I mean it. Sometimes I just feel like sitting down by myself where no one else can see and having a good cry."

"Mother, look..."

"You have no idea the things I have to go through with that man."

He took a deep breath and looked out at the parking lot. Up ahead he saw his car standing in profile in the sun.

"You just can't begin to imagine the torment..."

"Mother, excuse me. Would you mind stopping here for a second? It's such a warm day, I want to lock my coat in the car."

"Why, where did that beautiful thing come from?" she said, apparently noticing the coat for the first time. "Isn't that lovely." Her hand came over and stroked one sleeve. "So soft!"

"It's alpaca," Emmet said. "Helen surprised me with it last Christmas." He had actually quite strong feelings about the coat, because Helen had taken great care choosing it, and because when he had lifted it from the box Christmas morning she had kissed him fondly and then joked that she had always pictured herself married to a man who wore an alpaca topcoat.

"Wasn't that rather extravagant of her?" his mother asked, frankly critical. "Why a garment like this must cost several hundred dollars."

"Well, Mother, we can af..." He stopped, then realized it was too late to repair this second mistake and went on: "...afford a few nice things now, what with young Emmet's finally finishing college and the way the market's been acting lately."

"Can you?"

"A few. That's not to say we've begun acting like drunken..."

"Which car is yours, dear?"

"...sailors."

"The Ford there?"

"No, uh, the dark blue one beside it," he said, and pointed guiltily at his new Bentley sedan.

"That? Why, that's the biggest thing I've ever seen."

"Oh, no. Actually they make much larger ones," he said stupidly.

"Do they? I can hardly imagine," she returned, and gave him a bright, steadfast smile so redolent of resentment that he had to turn away again. "I had no idea you were doing so well," she said behind him.

"Well, the market and all," he said, repeating himself idiotically.

"It must be such a comfort."

"In a way, yes..."

"So nice for Helen. Women really need to feel secure."

"Helen..."

"Especially getting on into the fifties. A sense of security becomes so terribly important."

"Yes."

"A nice home and everything."

"Yes. You're right."

"Frankly, now that you're doing so well, I'm a little surprised you and Helen haven't considered giving up your apartment and buying a nice house somewhere. In the country maybe, with a little room to spread out."

Room enough to accommodate herself and his father was what she meant. It was an old lament, an old indictment, and while he had never learned how not to feel guilty hearing it delivered, he had at least developed some workable rejoinders – notably, pretending not to grasp her underlying meaning: "The truth is, Mother, with James married and Emmet Junior out of school now, the apartment is just fine for the two of us."

"Still, dear..."

"And anyway," he went ahead quickly. "I'm not doing *that* well. I mean, buying a home these days is really an enormous undertaking."

"But if you can afford a great big car like that..."

"Why, the down payment alone..."

"...and all kinds of expensive clothes."

"Actually, a man my age has no business saddling himself with a fifteen- or twenty-year mortgage."

"I see," she said, giving up suddenly.

"It wouldn't be fair to Helen, or the boys, or anyone," he went ahead anyway. "Do you realize I'm going to be fifty-eight years old next month? Why, that's way, way too late in life to start buying houses." All he said was true, but that didn't change how he felt saying it.

"It was only a suggestion," she returned, not looking at him now. "I only thought you and Helen might be happier in a bigger place."

"Of course, Mother, please don't think for an instant I don't appreciate your concern..."

"Anyway, you'd better hop out now and settle your coat so we can run on up to the house. Your father's going to be impossible as it is, and I don't want to aggravate the situation any more than I can help."

"I'll just be a second," Emmet said. But wanting to please her, he angled out of the cart too fast, banging his shins, and then, in his haste to rub them, dropped the topcoat on the pavement.

"Careful, Emmet," his mother called from behind. "You'll ruin your nice coat." And he thought again, God! If I could only just get *out* of here!

His father was in bed, stretched under the covers with only his face exposed. Emmet could see from the hall that his eyes were open and watching. But apparently he had something planned because as Emmet approached the bedroom door, he closed them and kept them closed, pretending to be asleep.

"Dad?" Emmet called softly from the end of the bed. "Dad? You awake?" His father had taken to playing peculiar games lately, and while they irritated Emmet in their foolishness, he still felt for some reason obliged to join in. "Dad?" he tried again softly. But his father refused to move.

Left alone, he considered for probably the fiftieth time the unnerving anomaly of new and old objects in his parents' bedroom: the sleek, low-slung twin beds, the Danish Modern dresser, the racy light fixtures, the two Paul Klee prints (surely not understood) that came with the lease. And intermingled, the silly, old-fashioned paraphernalia that came with his parents: a patchwork quilt lay over the electric blanket on his mother's bed, a photograph of himself as a child standing in a gilt, oval frame on the bleak surface of a Scandinavian night table, his grandmother Stennis's lace shawl folded across the arm of a

200

229 Old logo

230 New logo

231 Poster

232 The Old *Paris Match*

(229-233)
The redesign of *Paris Match* was a designer's fantasy. I was in Paris on business when the publisher, the remarkable eighty-seven year-old Jean Prouvost, "Patron" to his employees, asked me to redesign it. I was flattered and told him that I could have something in three or four months. He said, "You don't seem to understand I need it for tomorrow!" He really meant the next day. I couldn't resist the challenge and began redesigning the magazine together with a very cooperative art staff and editors. It was five-thirty on a Friday evening. We worked through until ten, broke for a few dozen oysters, and continued until two-thirty that morning. We resumed early Saturday, and worked straight through until eight in the evening. I started with the old logo, folded over the corner and put the word "Nouveau" on it. I told the editors that in America whenever the word "new" was put on a package, sales increased by twenty percent. Using the modified logotype not only on the cover, but also on posters and promotional material, I aimed at institutionalizing the new formula. I advised the staff not to always bleed their cover photographs and to use a simple and consistent style for their typographical headings. These changes, together with trimming three-quarters of an inch off the bottom, the magazine was strengthened, combined with an editorial product. The effect produced an impressive twenty percent increase in circulation. Of course, difficulty will be to sustain it.

202

234

235

I've taught at the School of Visual Arts for fifteen years. It has also provided an opportunity for me to produce some of my best work in the form of posters and announcements. The school's director, Dr. Silas Rhodes, has been an ideal client. All these posters were designed to be seen in the New York subways. They were aimed at young people, encouraging them to find out more about the school.

When I first began teaching about fifteen years ago, I taught from the point of view of developing the students' mastery of technique and understanding of styles. My assumption was that as a student developed strength and understanding, he could apply those skills to the task of self-expression. Now I teach from another perspective: I see the class as a voyage for students and teacher towards an uncharted goal. The trip is most useful in terms of personal growth. In other words, class problems are structured exactly reverse of the way I formerly taught. The class deals essentially with the students' personalities and obsessions (and mine). Technical skills emerge almost magically as a result of self-interest and practice.

203

Our faculty has
empathy, imagination, enthusiasm.
You benefit.

Department of Fine Arts: Painting, Drawing, Sculpture, Visual Perception, Printmaking

SCHOOL OF VISUAL ARTS

209 East 23rd Street. New York, New York 10010. OR 9-7350. Inquire: Office of Admissions

Department of Fine Arts: Painting, Drawing, Sculpture, Visual Perception, Printmaking

SCHOOL OF VISUAL ARTS

209 E. 23rd Street · New York, N.Y. 10010 · OR 9-7350 · Inquire: Office of Admissions

237

204

Film, Photography, Media Arts (Advertising, Illustration, Design, Fashion) Fine Arts, Video

OUR TIMES CALL FOR MULTIPLE CAREERS

School of Visual Arts
209 East 23rd Street, New York City 10010 / 679-7350

The School of Visual Arts

AN INDEPENDENT PROFESSIONAL ART SCHOOL IN HIGHER EDUCATION, 209 EAST 23RD STREET NEW YORK 10010

250 Courses

FILM, PHOTOGRAPHY, VIDEO TAPE, FINE ARTS, HUMANITIES, MEDIA ARTS.

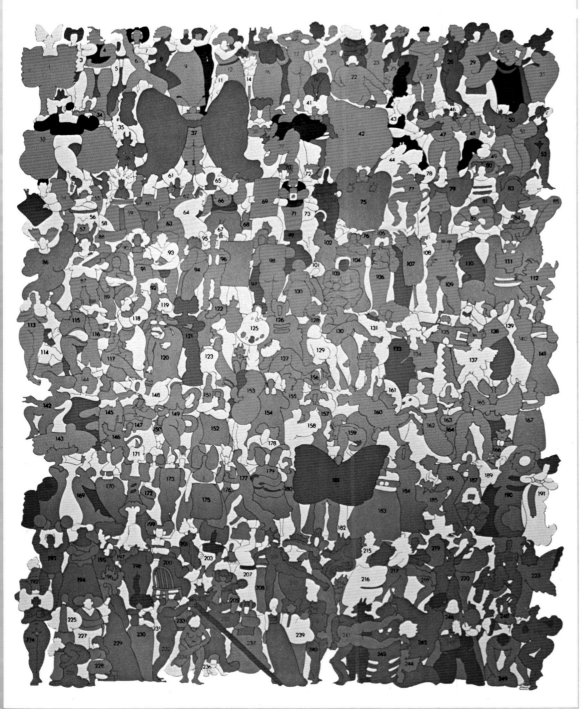

240

241

242

243

244

A record album can seem like an enormous area to work in after a diet of dust jackets and magazine covers. Because so many albums are bought on impulse, with the cover estimated at thirty to forty percent of the appeal factor, the manufacturers have heavily emphasized strong graphics. Because of the youth of the record-buying public, emphasis has been placed on innovative solutions.

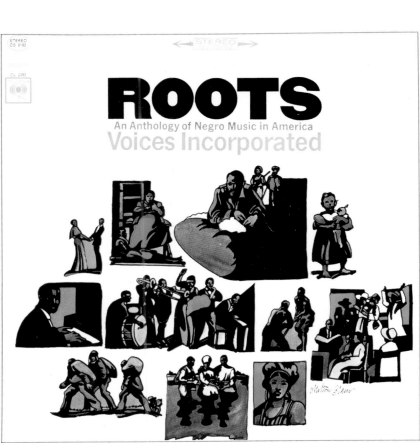

245

246

THE GEORGE LANG CORPORATION   160 CENTRAL PARK SO., NEW YORK 10019   212/CI 7-0300   EXT. 93-94   541-8070

G

247 For a food consultant.

605 MADISON AVENUE / NEW YORK, N.Y. 10022 / TEL. 212 759-7985

Bonnier International Design Ab

BURTON RICHARD WOLF

248 For a toy manufacturer.

ASTORIA PRESS INC., 435 HUDSON STREET, NEW YORK, N.Y. 10014   PRINTERS AND LITHOGRAPHERS   PHONE 255-6768

249 For a printer.

The Bear
295 Tinker Street/Boardville, New York 12409/Telephone (914) OR 9-7111

250 For an elegant restaurant.

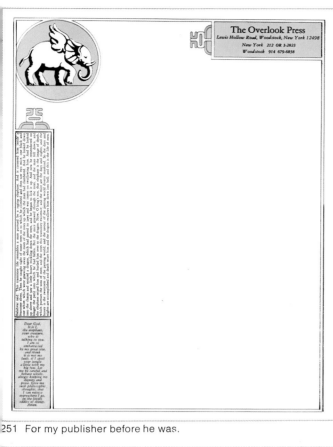

251 For my publisher before he was.

252 For my guru.

253 For an antique shop.

254 For Jean Michel Folon

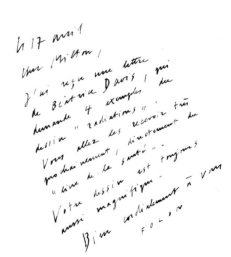

Folon's handwriting.

CD327 © 50c | Shakespeare | *The Signet Classic*

Henry V

CD326 © 50c | Shakespeare | *Tha Signet Classic*

The Comedy of Errors

CD174 © 50c | Shakespeare | *The Signet Classic*

The Tempest

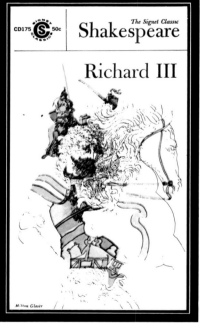

CD294 © 50c | Shakespeare | *The Signet Classic*

Pericles

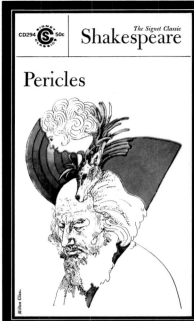

CD171 © 50c | Shakespeare | *Tha Signet Classic*

A Midsummer Night's Dream

CD331 © 50c | Shakespeare | *The Signet Classic*

The Taming of the Shrew

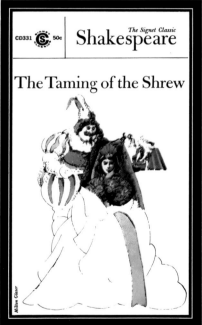

CD175 © 50c | Shakespeare | *The Signet Classic*

Richard III

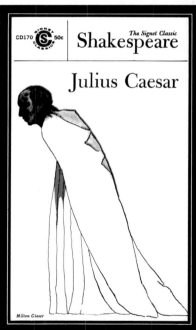

CD170 © 50c | Shakespeare | *Tha Signet Classic*

Julius Caesar

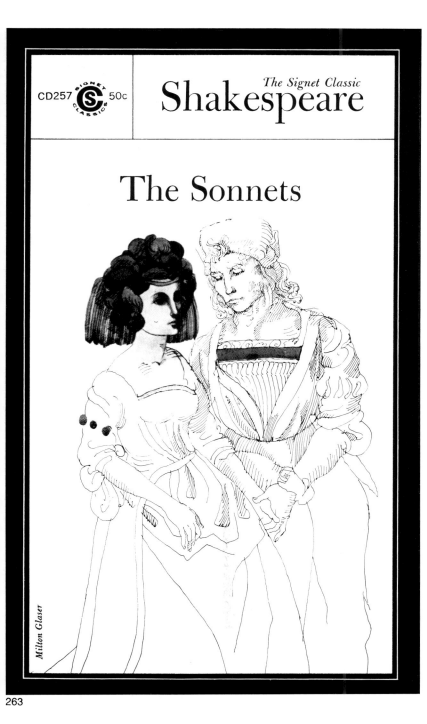

CD257 **50c** *The Signet Classic* **Shakespeare**

The Sonnets

Milton Glaser

(255-263)
A series of paperbacks which achieve their identity through a restricted use of color inside a black border. There are many competing versions of Shakespeare's plays and poetry in paperback, almost all executed in a very colorful way. Fifteen feet from a rack display these covers stand out like an island of white in a sea of color.

(264, 265)
These two album covers represent some of the earliest examples of a style now associated with me. It was a way of defining shapes with thin, black flowing lines; color was applied in broad, flat patterns. I was influenced by a variety of sources here—comic strips, Matisse, Persian painting, Japanese prints, but primarily the technique arose from the following situation: I was reaching a point in my work as an illustrator where it was becoming uneconomic to spend too much time on each drawing. I had to discover a way of working three or four times faster, without sacrificing either control or quality. Roughly at that time, transparent Cello-tac, a new art product was introduced. a wax-backed, adhesive color film that could be cut out with a razor blade, then rubbed down to adhere to a drawing. It was precisely the material I had been looking for. By first drawing outline, then indicating what areas were to be colored, I could, with assistance, triple my output. In early efforts the forms were **212** quite simple but, later, as in the example at the right, I began to deal more with interior modeling and more complex forms. My solution was similar to the one animators came to, faced with the problem of drawing tens of thousands of individual pictures. At the beginning, I thought there was something basically dishonest about this technique. But I got over that. At the time I think it may have saved my professional life.

264

265

266

267

(266, 267)
Left, a sketch for a foldout cover of *Time* (266), somewhat more interesting than the printed example below (267). There has been almost a ten-year span between the record albums on the opposite page and this *Time* cover. Ultimately, the style began to go stale and I found myself using it less and less.

(268-270)
Three other examples using the same technique applied to sports reporting and a newspaper ad introducing Fall programming for television.

268

269

(271-275)
Four studies (271-274) of
Elliot Gould, the American
movie actor, for a *Time* cover
(275). I rarely do more than
one preliminary drawing for
a job, but *Time* has a way of
making you nervous.

271

272

273

274

276

(276)
The typography for this fold-
out cover of *Life* leaves much
to be desired, but that is one
of the consequences of not
being in control of the total
surface. With *Life* I had no
choice over the style or position of the typography.

277

278

(277, 278)
The sketch (277) for this *Life* cover is superior, in its sense of scale and the quality of its drawing, to the final cover (278). I can't remember exactly what series of steps led to its weakening, but I do remember that it wasn't possible to show Dustin Hoffman drinking beer on the cover.

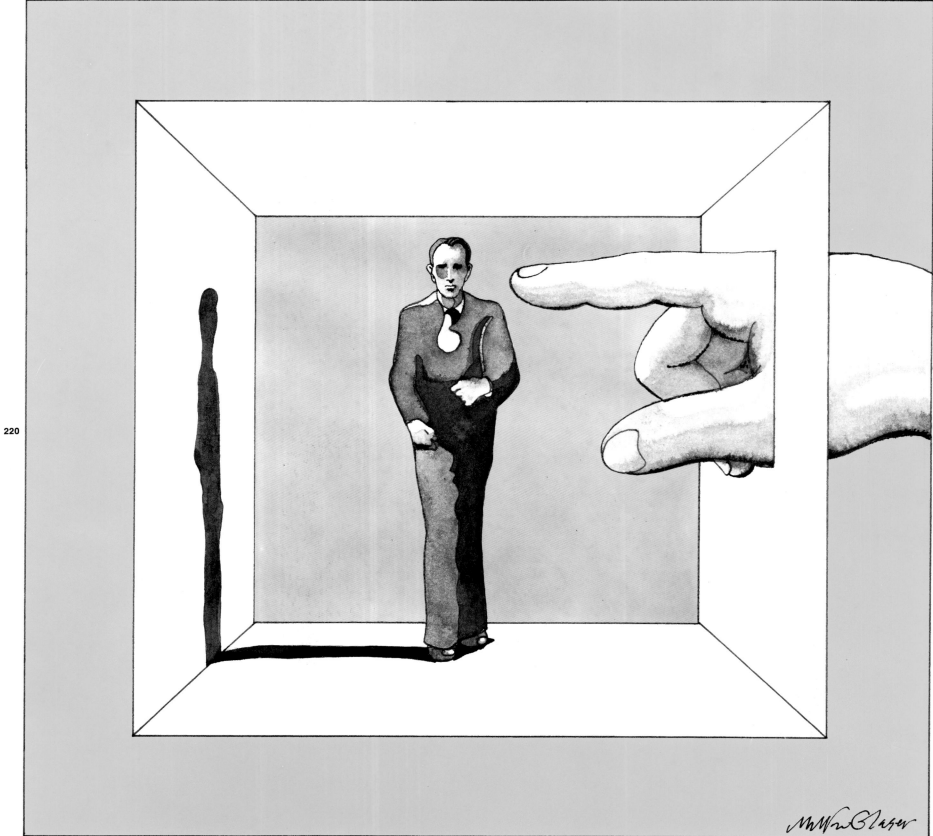

Peace Works

(279)
A symbol developed for the film *The Birthday Party* based on the Harold Pinter play. I was attempting to express three of Pinter's favorite themes—alienation, victimization, and paranoia.

(280)
A poster for an art show whose purpose was to support the effort to end the war in Vietnam.

(281-284)
This series of illustrations were done for a brochure promoting to firms the virtue of vocal computers.

221

Someday computers will talk.

(Welcome to Someday)

281

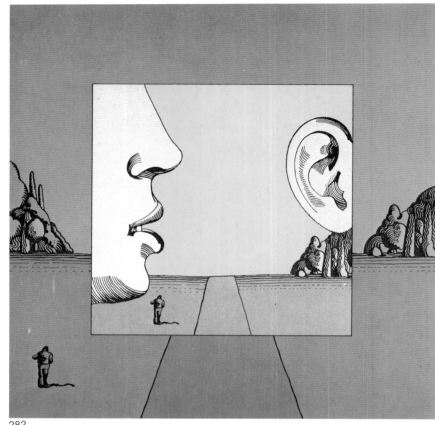

282

283

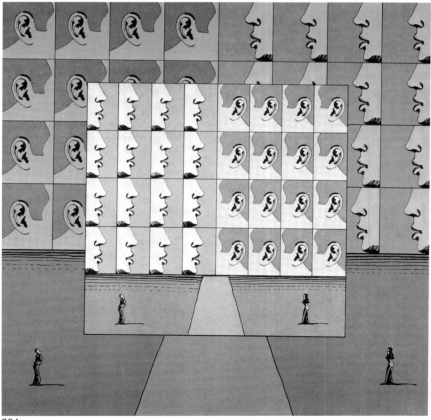

284

Lightnin'!

(285-288)
The Lightning Hopkins album cover (285, 286) on the two preceding pages are examples of dealing with two sides of a surface. The act of turning the surface produces an extra dimension. Perhaps this can be made clear by the examples on the right (287, 288). These two drawings appeared as right hand pages in magazines.

(289, 290)
The drawing at the bottom was about a girl's first experience with drugs. Turn the page and complete the visual story. Magazines and books provide an excellent vehicle for the exploration of time, since they yield a time experience as pages are turned. In fact, one recalls that one of the most pervasive clichés indicating the passage of time in movies shows calendar pages turning one by one. Magazines are frequently faced with the problem of maintaining reader interest over a number of pages. The storytelling graphic sequence is a very useful solution, drawn in large part from the time conventions of comics. How much of our perception of time has been affected by our exposure to comics and to a notion of time as a sequence of frozen images is difficult to determine. We do know that the influence on the designer's vocabulary, consciously or unconsciously, has been enormous.

287

288

289

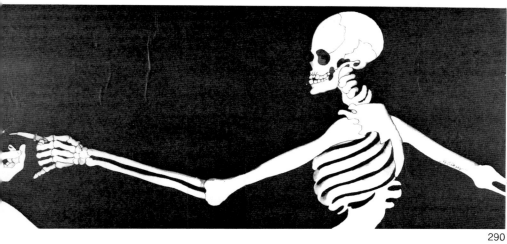

290

(291-293)
The sketch (292) and finish (291) for a food story that originally appeared in *Look*. The inspiration for this drawing came from a painting by Thomas Cole of a giant chalice in a landscape (293).
I simply changed the chalice to a grapefruit. It is sad to think that many of the magazines that I worked for (*Audience*, *Life*, the early *Show*, *Look*, *Eye*, among others) have all ceased publishing.

292

293

291

Fig. 104. *Notre Soleil est une gigantesque centrale nucléaire, qui fabrique en permanence toutes sortes de rayonnements. Nous sommes protégés de la plupart de ses rayonnements ionisants, qui seraient nocifs pour nous.*

294

(294)
I mentioned earlier that skulls
and skeletons are recurring
themes in my work. This example was done for a French
health book on the dangers
of solar radiation.

You Are What You Eat.

(295)
There is enormous satisfaction in excavating hidden imagery. This poster was done for a motion picture, but was never used. Although there are numerous examples of unpublished works in this book, I would say that on average ninety percent of my work is eventually used. I probably have psychological attachments to the ones that don't make it.

La Tempesta with a Schmata   M...Von Glaser May 29 1967

296

(296-300)
The following drawings were
based on a favorite painting
of mine, Giorgione's *The
Tempest* (297). I added another
element to the subject, a
crumpled rag.

297

299

(301-302)
The sketch (301) and the
final silkscreen poster (302)
were commissioned by
The Paris Review to raise
money for this interesting
literary magazine.

234

301

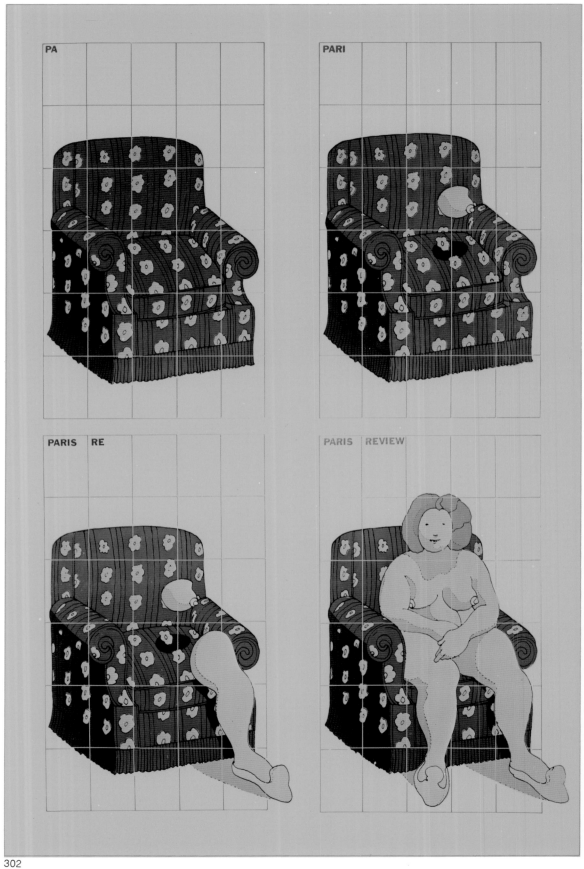

302

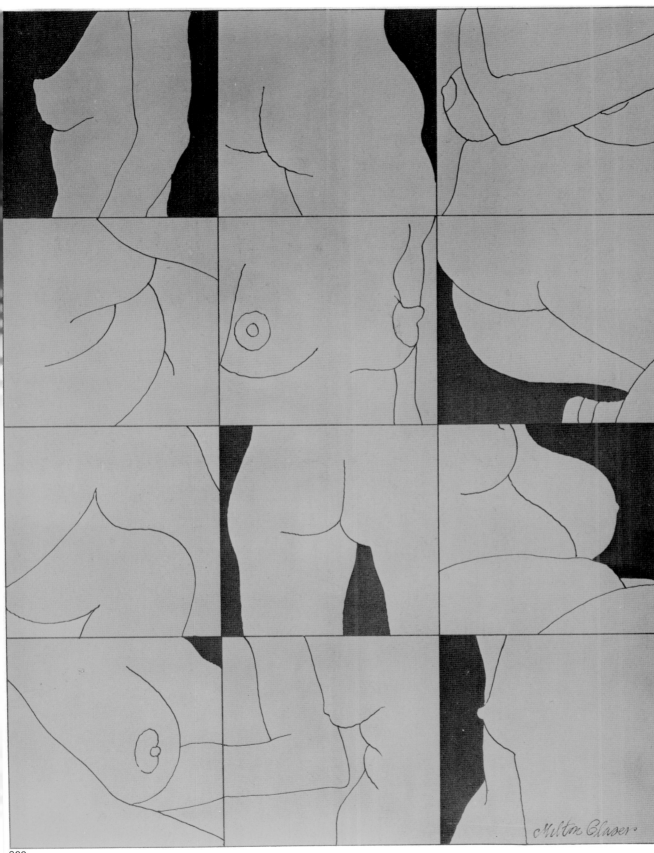

(303)
A page of nudes that ap-
peared in the *Graphic*.

235

(304-309)
I was hired by a movie company for the ideal assignment: to illustrate a brochure promoting a film that the Italian director Visconti was making of Thomas Mann's *Death in Venice*. For two weeks I stayed at a great hotel, the Cipriani, ate fabulous food, sketched every day, and observed the production in progress. I've always had deep associations with Venice from my first visit as a student. I was also deeply moved by Mann's dark sense of the city. The sketch I did of the Bridge of Sighs served as an inspiration for the brochure cover. The inside of the brochure follows on the next two pages.

· 304

short, an impulse to flight surged in
him. "My heart needs to question
the world," he declares to his friend
Alfried, "to find a place where I
can lose myself and contemplate
my life and my destiny without
disturbance."

What Aschenbach cannot guess is
that this fabulous, magic, foreign
place to which he comes seeking
renewed life, hoping to find his inspiration again, conceals his ruin.
Yet the hints are there. Premoni-
tions on every side of him: in the
grotesque figure of the young-old
man on the steamer to Venice, playing the buffoon, babbling, bowing
and scraping to hold the attention
of the youths; in the brutish, mut-
tering gondolier, who runs off
without his pay; and in the glimpse
of a diseased man slumping to a
lonely death in the midst of a busy
railway station....

The haunting story from the
masterpiece of the great German
writer, Thomas Mann, lives in
every nuance in the hands of its
Italian director. Luchino Visconti
has touched the very source of
Mann's inspiration, even to recreat-
ing Aschenbach as a composer.
Mann, much affected by the death
that summer of the famous
musician Mahler, whom he had
known briefly in Munich, sketched

306

There were long dry Americans,
large-familied Russians, English
ladies, German children with
French bonnes. The Slavic element
predominated.

Near him sits a group of young
people speaking Polish: three girls,
their governess, and a lad of fourteen. At once, Aschenbach is struck
by him, fascinated by the boy's
perfect beauty. A beauty that sum-
mons up the noblest moment of
Greek sculpture.

Tadzio, for so he's called, wears an
expression of pure serenity, revealing a chaste perfection of form
that Aschenbach had never seen
consummated so happily in nature
or in art. The image of beauty,
the very soul of classical simplicity
and symmetry...

It was the head of Eros with the
yellowish bloom of Parian marble,
with fine serious brows....The
head was poised like a flower, in
incomparable loveliness...
Such beauty in a human being?
Here in Venice—that city of many
crossroads, that floating dream,
that rich mingling of races and
cultures, a city which seems history
itself—Aschenbach had found a
likeness, beauty's essence, so rare

307

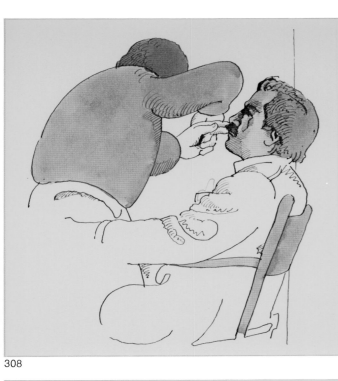

The piazzas are suddenly quite deserted, and the stench of disinfectant penetrates everywhere. Baffled and desperate, Aschenbach tries to learn the cause. His questions are rebuffed by the hotel manager, the barber, and ridiculed by the strolling street musician, whose sinister song makes the other guests roar with laughter as though possessed by some demon. There are whispers, there are denials, but the fact is that pestilence has gripped the city. And though the officials continue to reject reports that people are dying of cholera, the disease is seething through the now feverish body of the city.

Finally, the truth is revealed reluctantly to him by the Englishman in the travel office. He warns that disease and corruption run together in Venice: there are surly gangs in the streets, drunkenness, licentiousness, and always the fear of the walking terror, the cholera. "Go, leave now, today," urges the Englishman, "for the quarantine cannot be more than a few days off." Aschenbach longs to cry out to Tadzio and his family—save yourselves! Yet he is powerless. He vacillates, agonizing in the fear of losing forever the stranger god he adores. Like a criminal, he now

must keep hidden the city's calamitous secret as well as his own. Beyond all help, and altogether lost to shame, he livens his appearance with smart ties and succumbs to the barber's ministrations that make him look young again—a young-old man not much different from the revolting buffoon on the steamer.

"The time left us is like hour-glass sand," he has told a friend, "to our eyes it appears to run out only in the end." The thought of his former life of reason and self-mastery makes him wince in revulsion. He must keep silent, stay on, and live this brief time left him, moment by moment.

For in the delirium of his passion, he has glimpsed what few men are fortunate enough to see: the divine beauty incarnate.

So to the very end, Aschenbach sits and gazes desperately at Tadzio, and the lad smiles at him, beckoning like a pale and lovely summoner from the Adriatic...which seems now the waters of eternity.

Some minutes passed before anyone hastened to the aid of the elderly man sitting there collapsed in his chair. They bore him to his room. And before nightfall a shocked and respectful world received the news of his decease.

(1)
Subject: From Poppy with Love
Description: Poster
Client: Poppy Records
Art Directors: Milton Glaser / Kevin Eggers
Technique: Water Color

(2)
Subject: Art Deco
Description: Poster
Client: Cranbrook Academy
Technique: Line

(3)
Subject: Art Deco
Description: Magazine Cover
Client: Print Magazine
Art Director: Andrew Kner
Photographer: Peggy Barnett
Technique: Three-dimensional Assembly

(4-6)
Subject: Bach
Description: Poster and Details
Client: Columbia Records
Art Director: John Berg
Technique: Water Color

(7)
Subject: Ear in Tree
Description: Poster
Client: National Academy of Recording
        Arts and Sciences
Art Director: Bob Cato
Technique: Water Color

(8)
Subject: New Year's Greeting
Description: Poster
Client: Savage-Friedman
Art Director: Lee Savage
Technique: Ink

(9)
Subject: Aretha Franklin
Description: Poster
Client: Eye Magazine
Art Director: Alfred Celzer
Technique: Cello-Tak

(10)
Subject: Joan Baez
Description: Poster (Unpublished)
Client: Vanguard Records
Technique: Colored Ink

(11)
Subject: Thérèse
Description: Paperback Cover
Client: Farrar, Straus & Giroux
Art Director: Hal Vursell
Technique: Pen, Ink, and Wash

(12)
Subject: Ché Guevara
Description: Magazine Illustration
Client: Ramparts Magazine
Art Director: Dugald Stermer
Technique: Colored Ink

(13)
Subject: Jack Ruby
Description: Magazine Illustration
Client: Ramparts Magazine
Art Director: Dugald Stermer
Technique: Colored Ink and Cello-Tak

(14)
Subject: Oscar Wilde
Description: Magazine Cover
Client: Push Pin Graphic
Art Directors: Milton Glaser / Seymour Chwast
Technique: Pencil

(15, 16)
Subject: Marquis de Sade
Description: Magazine Cover
Client: Push Pin Graphic
Art Directors: Milton Glaser / Seymour Chwast
Technique: Sepia Wash

(17)
Subject: Walt Whitman
Description: Magazine Illustration
Client: Vista Magazine
Art Director: Richard Hess
Technique: Pen and Ink

(18)
Subject: Self-portrait
Description: Drawing
Technique: Crayon

(19)
Subject: Socrates
Description: Magazine Illustration
Client: Look Magazine
Art Director: Alan Hurlburt
Technique: Colored Paper Cutout
          and Wash Drawing

(20)
Subject: W. C. Fields
Description: Paperback Cover
Client: Warner Paperback Library
Art Director: Harris Lewine
Technique: Pen and Ink

(21-25)
Subject: Hesse
Description: Paperback Cover Series
Client: Farrar, Straus & Giroux
Art Director: Hal Vursell
Technique: Line

(26, 27)
Subject: Puerto Rican Portraits
Description: Magazine Illustration
Client: New York Magazine
Art Directors: Milton Glaser / Walter Bernard
Technique: Pencil

(28-31)
Subject: Various Heads
Description: Promotion Booklet
Client: Sanders Printing
Art Directors: Milton Glaser / Seymour Chwast
Technique: Pen, Ink, Pencil, and Wash

(32)
Subject: Steppenwolf
Description: Book Jacket
Client: Modern Library
Art Director: Tere LoPrete
Technique: Pen, Ink, and Wash

(33)
Subject: e.e. cummings
Description: Paperback Cover
Client: E.P. Dutton
Art Director: Cy Nelson
Technique: Pen and Ink

(34)
Subject: Napoleon
Description: Paperback Cover
Client: New American Library
Art Director: Bill Gregory
Technique: Pen and Ink

(35)
Subject: The Face of Jesus
Description: Magazine Illustration
Client: Esquire Magazine
Art Director: Bob Benton
Technique: Photographic Assembly

(36)
Subject: Drug Skull
Description: Magazine Illustration
Client: Vista Magazine
Art Director: Richard Hess
Technique: Water Color

(37)
Subject: Welcome to the Club
Description: Book Jacket
Client: McGraw-Hill
Art Director: Al Cetta
Technique: Pen and Ink

(38)
Reference for Plate 39

(39)
Subject: Bob Dylan
Description: Poster
Client: Columbia Records
Art Director: Bob Cato
Technique: Ink and Cello-Tak

(40-43)
Subject: Mahalia Jackson
Description: Poster
Client: Gary Keys
Art Director: Gary Keys
Technique: Wash

(44, 45)
Subject: Music Festival
Description: Posters
Client: Temple University
Art Director: Ann Boehlan
Technique: Pen and Ink

(46)
Subject: Russian Tea Room
Description: Poster
Client: Russian Tea Room
Art Directors: Milton Glaser
              Faith Stewart Gordon
Technique: Wash

(47)
Subject: Toys by Artists
Description: Poster
Client: Bonniers International
Art Directors: Milton Glaser / Burton Wolf
Technique: Pen, Ink, and Color Wash

(48)
Subject: Dada and Surrealism
Description: Poster (Sketch)
Client: The Museum of Modern Art
Technique: Ballpoint

(49)
Subject: Dada and Surrealism
Description: Poster (Unpublished)
Client: The Museum of Modern Art
Technique: Cello-Tak

(50)
Subject: Fly Head
Description: Magazine Illustration
Client: Show Magazine
Art Director: Henry Wolf
Technique: Pen and Ink

(51, 52)
Subject: Don Giovanni
Description: Album Cover and Detail
Client: Columbia Records
Art Director: John Berg
Technique: Pen and Ink

(53)
Subject: Mother and Child
Description: Magazine Cover
Client: Push Pin Graphic
Art Directors: Milton Glaser / Seymour Chwast
Technique: Pen and Ink

(54)
Subject: Leda
Description: Album Cover
Client: Poppy Records
Art Directors: Milton Glaser / Kevin Eggers
Technique: Pen and Ink

(55)
Subject: Mourning Dog
Description: Drawing for Poster
Client: Olivetti Corporation
Art Director: Giorgio Soavi
Technique: Pen and Ink

(56)
Subject: Devil Head
Description: Movie Symbol (Unpublished)
Client: Maysles Brothers
Technique: Pen and Ink

(57-62)
Subject: Asimov's Annotated Don Juan
Description: Book Illustration and Sketches
Client: Doubleday
Art Director: Alex Gotfryd
Technique: Pen, Ink, and Wash

(63)
Subject: The Hive
Description: Book Jacket
Client: Farrar, Straus & Giroux
Art Director: Hal Vursell
Technique: Pen and Ink

(64)
Subject: Pierre, or the Ambiguities
Description: Paperback Cover
Client: New American Library
Art Director: Bill Gregory
Technique: Pen, Ink, and Colored Wash

(65, 66)
Subject: Leaning Man
Description: Magazine Illustration
Client: Audience Magazine
Art Directors: Milton Glaser / Seymour Chwast
              Vincent Ceci
Technique: Pen, Ink, and Cello-Tak

(67)
Subject: Elephant
Description: Pharmaceutical Brochure
Client: B. H. Robbins Vitamins
Technique: Pen, Ink, and Colored Wash

(68)
Subject: Coffee Pot
Description: Magazine Illustration
Client: Signature Magazine
Art Director: David Olin
Technique: Pen, Ink, and Cello-Tak

(69)
Subject: Poppy Foot
Description: Poster
Client: Poppy Records
Art Directors: Milton Glaser / Kevin Eggers
Technique: Water Color

(70)
Subject: Soccer Game
Description: Magazine Illustration
Client: Sports Illustrated Magazine
Art Director: Dick Gangel
Technique: Water Color

(71)
Subject: Nijinsky
Description: Magazine Illustration
Client: Audience Magazine
Art Directors: Milton Glaser / Seymour Chwast
              Vincent Ceci
Technique: Water Color

(72)
Subject: Abortionist
Description: Magazine Illustration
Client: Ramparts Magazine
Art Director: Dugald Stermer
Technique: Water Color

(73)
Subject: Spoon River Anthology
Description: Paperback Cover
Client: Harper and Row
Art Director: Margo Herr
Technique: Water Color

(74)
Subject: e. e. cummings
Description: Magazine Cover
Client: Push Pin Graphic
Art Directors: Milton Glaser / Seymour Chwast
Technique: Wash

(75)
Subject: Pregnant Woman
Description: Magazine Cover
Client: Push Pin Graphic
Art Directors: Milton Glaser / Seymour Chwast
Technique: Wash

(76)
Subject: Shadowlight Theater
Description: Poster
Client: The School of Visual Arts
Art Director: Silas Rhodes
Technique: Wash

(77)
Subject: Artists at Work
Description: Drawing
Technique: Wash

(78-81)
Subject: The Devil's Pi
Description: Promotional Booklet
Client: Composing Room
Art Director: Dr. Robert Leslie
Technique: Wash

(82)
Subject: Don Quixote
Description: Album Cover
Client: Columbia Records
Art Director: Bob Cato
Technique: Wash

(83)
Subject: The Cook
Description: Book Jacket

Client: Holt, Rhinehart and Winston
Art Director: Tere LoPrete
Technique: Wash

(84-87)
Subject: Follies
Description: Magazine Illustration
Client: Push Pin Graphic
Art Director: Milton Glaser
Technique: Wash and Mechanical Dots

(88-91)
Subject: Nudes
Description: Book Illustration (Unpublished)
Technique: Pen, Ink, and Wash

(92-97)
Subject: Méliès
Description: Magazine Illustration
Client: Push Pin Graphic
Art Director: Milton Glaser
Technique: Pen and Ink

(98-103)
Subject: Cats and Bats and Things with Wings
Description: Book Design and Illustration
Client: Atheneum
Art Director: Harry Ford
Technique: Pen, Ink, and Wash

(104-107)
Subject: The Dream Book
Description: Magazine Illustration
Client: Push Pin Graphic
Art Directors: Milton Glaser / Seymour Chwast
Technique: Pen and Ink

(108)
Subject: The Mutilation of Tennessee Williams
Description: Magazine Illustration
Client: Esquire Magazine
Art Director: Sam Antupit
Technique: Wash Conversion

(109)
Subject: Fish in the Sky
Description: Book Design and Illustration
Client: Doubleday
Art Director: Alex Gotfryd
Technique: Water Color

(110-112)
Subject: Burning Potato
Description: Album Cover
Client: Poppy Records
Art Directors: Milton Glaser / Kevin Eggers
Photographer: Peggy Barnett
Technique: Photography

(113, 116)
Subject: Zimm's Palette
Description: Magazine Cover
Client: Graphis Magazine
Art Director: Walter Herdeg
Technique: Crayon

(114, 115)
Subject: Zimm's Palette
Description: Drawings (Unpublished)
Technique: Crayon

(117-121)
Subject: Amphetamine Story
Description: Magazine Illustration
Client: New York Magazine
Art Directors: Milton Glaser / Walter Bernard
Technique: Pen, Ink, and Cello-Tak

(122)
Subject: Funco File
Description: Book Jacket
Client: Doubleday
Art Director: Alex Gotfryd
Lettering: George Leavitt
Technique: Pen, Ink, and Cello-Tak

(123)
Subject: The Underground Gourmet
Description: Paperback Cover
Client: Simon and Schuster
Art Director: Frank Metz
Technique: Pen and Ink

(124)
Subject: WCBS/FM
Description: Poster
Client: WCBS/FM
Art Director: Dale Fon
Technique: Pencil, Crayon, Pen, Ink,
          and Water Color

(125)
Subject: Big Nude
Description: Poster
Client: The School of Visual Arts
Art Director: Silas Rhodes
Technique: Line

(126)
Subject: Brubeck and Basie
Description: Poster
Client: Gary Keys
Art Director: Gary Keys
Technique: Pen and Ink

(127)
Subject: Surrealism
Description: Book Jacket (Unpublished)
Client: E. P. Dutton
Art Director: Cy Nelson
Technique: Pen, Ink, and Wash

(128, 129)
Subject: John Dickson Carr
Description: Book Jacket
Client: Macmillan
Art Director: Harris Lewine
Technique: Colored Ink and Cello-Tak

(130)
Subject: A Delicate Balance
Description: Paperback Cover
Client: Pocket Books
Art Director: Sol Immerman
Technique: Ink

(131)
Subject: Everything in the Garden
Description: Paperback Cover
Client: Pocket Books
Art Director: Sol Immerman
Technique: Pen and Ink

(132)
Subject: Dead Corse
Description: Paperback Cover
Client: Avon Books
Art Director: Barbara Bertoli
Technique: Pen, Ink, and Cello-Tak

(133)
Subject: One Man Show
Description: Paperback Cover
Client: Avon Books
Art Director: Barbara Bertoli
Illustrator: Roger Hane
Technique: Acrylic

(134)
Subject: Bite
Description: Book Jacket
Client: Norton
Art Director: Hugh O'Neill
Technique: Pen and Ink

(135)
Subject: Hunger
Description: Book Jacket
Client: Farrar, Straus & Giroux
Art Director: Hal Vursell
Technique: Pen and Ink

(136)
Subject: The Chocolate Deal
Description: Book Jacket
Client: Holt, Rhinehart and Winston
Art Director: Harris Lewine
Technique: Pen and Ink

(137)
Subject: Futz
Description: Brochure Cover
Client: Commonwealth United
Technique: Three-dimensional Assembly

(138)
Subject: The School of Visual Arts
Description: Catalogue Cover
Client: The School of Visual Arts
Art Director: Silas Rhodes
Technique: Cut Paper

(139)
Subject: Gog
Description: Book Jacket
Client: Macmillan
Art Director: Abe Lerner
Book Photographed by Claudine Vernier
Technique: Pen and Ink

(140)
Subject: Lord Jim
Description: Book Jacket
Client: Doubleday
Art Director: Alex Gotfryd
Lettering: George Leavitt
Technique: Pen and Ink

(141)
Subject: Art Nouveau Bathing Beauty
Description: Magazine Cover
Client: Holiday Magazine
Art Director: Frank Zachary
Technique: Pen and Ink

(142-153)
Subjects: California
          Twen
          Chicago
          Inside the Big Apple
          Combine Works
          The Poison Pen
          Milanese Graphics
          The Landscape
          1 Print 1 Painting
          Concrete Poetry
          Robert Delpire
          VanDerBeek
Description: Gallery Announcements
Client: The School of Visual Arts
Art Director: Silas Rhodes
Technique: Pen and Ink

(154, 155)
Subject: Transparency
Description: Gallery Announcement and Sketch
Client: The School of Visual Arts
Art Director: Silas Rhodes
Technique: Pen and Ink

(156)
Subject: Man Walking on Staircase
Description: Journal Cover
Client: The American Institute of Graphic Arts
Art Director: Ed Gottschall
Photographs: Muybridge
Technique: Photographic Assembly

(157, 158)
Subject: Staircase Variations and Sketch
Description: Magazine Cover
Client: Idea Magazine
Art Director: Hiroshi Ohchi
Technique: Pen, Ink, and Wash

(159)
Subject: Greta Garbo
Description: Book Jacket
Client: McGraw-Hill
Art Director: Harris Lewine
Lettering: George Leavitt
Technique: Photography, Pen and Ink

(160, 161)
Subject: Babyfat
Description: Type Face Design
Lettering Execution: George Leavitt

(162, 163)
Subject: Simon and Garfunkel
Description: Poster and Sketch
Client: Gary Keys
Art Director: Gary Keys
Technique: Pen, Ink, and Wash

(164)
Reference for Plate 165

(165)
Subject: Babyteeth
Description: Type Face Design
Lettering Execution: George Leavitt

(166, 167)
Subject: Hugh Masekela
Description: Poster and Sketch
Client: Gary Keys
Art Director: Gary Keys
Technique: Pen, Ink, and Wash

(168, 169)
Subject: Neo Futura
Description: Type Face Design
Client: Photolettering
Lettering Execution: George Leavitt

(170)
Subject: Response Ability

Description: Logotype
Client: The Art Directors Club
        Communications Conference

(171)
Subject: B
Description: Logotype
Client: Beylarian

(172)
Subject: Performance
Description: Logotype
Client: The International Design
        Conference in Aspen, 1973

(173, 174)
Subject: Houdini
Description: Type Face Design
Client: Photolettering
Lettering Execution: George Leavitt

(175)
Subject: Chinese Grocery
Description: Poster
Client: The International Design
        Conference in Aspen, 1973
Photographer: Steve Myers
Technique: Photography

(176)
Subject: Festifilms
Description: Promotion Design
Client: New Audiences
Art Director: Art Wiener
Technique: Pen, Ink, and Cello-Tak

(177)
Subject: Babycurls
Description: Type Face Design
Client: Photolettering
Lettering Execution: George Leavitt

(178)
Subject: Lamp
Description: Detail from Poster
Client: The School of Visual Arts
Art Director: Silas Rhodes
Photographer: Alan Vogel
Technique: Three-dimensional Assembly

(179-185)
Subject: Toy Store
Description: Architectural Design
Client: Childcraft
Photographer: Norman McGrath

(186)
Subject: L Blocks
Description: Toy Design
Client: Bonniers International
Art Director: Burton Wolf
Photographer: Peggy Barnett
Technique: Plastic Construction

(187)
Subject: Cubismo
Description: Toy Design
Client: George Beylarian
Technique: Molded Plastic

(188)
Subject: Palette
Description: Three-dimensional Painting
Client: The School of Visual Arts
Art Director: Silas Rhodes
Photographer: Alan Vogel
Technique: Three-dimensional Assembly
          and Acrylic

(189)
Subject: The Rasputin
Description: Cocktail Design
Client: Russian Tea Room
Art Director: Faith Stewart Gordon
Drink Photographed by Claudine Vernier
Technique: A Little Bit of Clam Juice,
          Lots of Vodka, a Slice of Lemon,
          and an Anchovy Olive

(190, 191, 194)
Subject: Logo, Menu, Match Box
Description: Promotion Design
Client: Russian Tea Room
Art Director: Faith Stewart Gordon
Technique: Pen and Ink

(192, 193)
Subject: Postcards
Description: Promotion Design
Client: Russian Tea Room
Art Director: Faith Stewart Gordon
Technique: Pen, Ink, and Cello-Tak

(195)
Subject: Illuminated Flag
Description: Lamp Design (Unproduced)
Lamp Photographed by Claudine Vernier
Technique: Plastic and Light Bulbs

(196)
Subject: The National Standard
Description: Book Jacket
Client: Holt, Rhinehart and Winston
Art Director: Harris Lewine
Technique: Photography

(197-203)
Subject: Jackson Pollock
Description: Book Jacket
Client: McGraw-Hill
Art Director: Harris Lewine

(204, 205)
Subject: Bread Studies
Description: Drawings
Client: American Institute of Graphic Arts:
Survival Show
Technique: Water Color

(206)
Subject: Bread
Description: Sculpture
Client: American Institute of Graphic Arts:
Survival Show
Sculpture Photographed by Claudine Vernier
Technique: Nickel-plated Bread

(207-219)
Description: Editorial Design
Client: New York Magazine
Art Directors: Milton Glaser / Walter Bernard

(220)
Subject: Mountain Range
Description: Magazine Cover
Client: Audience Magazine
Art Directors: Milton Glaser / Seymour Chwast
Vincent Ceci
Photographer: Jay Maisel
Technique: Photography

(221)
Subject: Car Front
Description: Magazine Cover
Client: Audience Magazine
Art Directors: Milton Glaser / Seymour Chwast
Vincent Ceci
Photographer: Steve Myers
Technique: Photography

(222)
Subject: Shoes
Description: Magazine Cover
Client: Audience Magazine
Art Directors: Milton Glaser / Seymour Chwast
Vincent Ceci
Illustrator: Barbara Nessim
Technique: Pen, Ink, and Wash

(223-228)
Subjects: Notes from Inner Space
Car Customizing
How I Had Nothing to Do with the Movie Version
but What I Think of it Anyway
City Rat
Conversation: Arthur Miller and William Styron
Geritol Days of Lawrence Welk
Description: Editorial Design
Client: Audience Magazine
Art Directors: Milton Glaser / Seymour Chwast
Vincent Ceci
Photographers: Steve Myers (224)
Steve Salmieri (226)

(229-235)
Description: Editorial Design

Client: Paris Match
Art Director: Paul Pignot

(236)
Subject: Our Faculty Has Empathy, Imagination,
Enthusiasm. You Benefit.
Description: Poster
Client: The School of Visual Arts
Art Director: Silas Rhodes
Photographer: Sol Mednick
Technique: Painted Sculpture

(238)
Subject: Our Times Call for Multiple Careers
Description: Poster
Client: The School of Visual Arts
Art Director: Silas Rhodes
Technique: Wash

(237)
Subject: Palette
Description: Poster
Client: The School of Visual Arts
Art Director: Silas Rhodes
Photographer: Alan Vogel
Technique: Three-dimensional Assembly
and Acrylic

(239)
Subject: 250 Courses
Description: Poster
Client: The School of Visual Arts
Art Director: Silas Rhodes
Technique: Pen and Ink

(240)
Subject: The Mandrake Memorial
Description: Album Cover
Client: Poppy Records
Art Directors: Milton Glaser / Kevin Eggers
Technique: Pencil and Colored Inks

(241)
Subject: Two Harpsichords
Description: Album Cover
Client: Columbia Records
Art Director: Ron Coro
Technique: Crayon, Tempera, Cello-Tak,
and Pencil

(242)
Subject: Son Nova 1988
Description: Album Cover
Client: Son Nova Records
Technique: Cutout

(243)
Subject: Doc Watson
Description: Album Cover
Client: Poppy Records
Art Directors: Milton Glaser / Kevin Eggers
Technique: Water Color

(244)
Subject: Aaron Lightman
Description: Album Cover
Client: Poppy Records
Art Directors: Milton Glaser / Kevin Eggers
Technique: Water Color

(245)
Subject: Erik Von Schmidt
Description: Album Cover
Client: Poppy Records
Art Directors: Milton Glaser / Kevin Eggers
Photographer: Unknown Army Photographer
Technique: Pen, Ink, and Cello-Tak

(246)
Subject: Roots
Description: Album Cover
Client: Columbia Records
Art Director: John Berg
Technique: Water Color

(247)
Subject: Food Consultant
Description: Letterhead
Client: George Lang
Technique: Pen and Ink

(248)
Subject: Toy Manufacturer
Description: Letterhead
Client: Bonniers International

(249)
Subject: Printer
Description: Letterhead
Client: Astoria Press

(250)
Subject: The Bear Restaurant
Description: Letterhead
Client: Albert Grossman
Technique: Pen and Ink

(251)
Subject: Publisher
Description: Letterhead
Client: The Overlook Press
Technique: Pen and Ink

(252)
Subject: Oriental Art Store
Description: Letterhead
Client: Rudi Oriental Antiques

(253)
Subject: Antique Shop
Description: Letterhead
Client: The Real Tinsel
Technique: Pen and Ink

(254)
Subject: Personal Stationery
Description: Letterhead
Client: Jean Michel Folon

(255-263)
Subject: Shakespeare Plays
Description: Paperback Cover Series
Client: New American Library
Art Director: Bill Gregory
Technique: Pen, Ink, and Water Color

(264, 265)
Subjects: Sound of Chicago, Volume II
Sound of New Orleans, Volume I
Description: Album Covers
Client: Columbia Records
Art Director: John Berg
Technique: Pen, Ink, and Cello-Tak

(266, 267)
Subject: California
Description: Magazine Cover and Sketch
Client: Time Magazine
Art Director: Lou Glessmann
Technique: Pen, Ink, and Cello-Tak

(268)
Subject: Tennis Match
Description: Promotional Brochure
Client: Champion Papers
Art Director: Jim Miho
Technique: Cello-Tak

(269)
Subject: Orange Bowl Football Game
Description: Magazine Illustration
Client: Sports Illustrated Magazine
Art Director: Dick Gangle
Technique: Cello-Tak

(270)
Subject: TV Show on America
Description: Newspaper Ad (Unpublished)
Client: CBS
Art Director: Lou Dorfsman
Technique: Pen, Ink, and Wash

(271-274)
Subject: Elliott Gould
Description: Magazine Cover Studies
Client: Time Magazine
Art Director: Lou Glessmann
Technique: Pen, Ink, and Wash

(275)
Subject: Elliott Gould
Description: Magazine Cover
Client: Time Magazine
Art Director: Lou Glessmann
Technique: Pen, Ink, and Wash

(276)
Subject: American Indian
Description: Magazine Cover
Client: Life Magazine

Art Director: Bernie Quint
Technique: Pen, Ink, and Cello-Tak

(277, 278)
Subject: John Wayne and Dustin Hoffman
Description: Magazine Cover and Sketch
Client: Life Magazine
Art Director: Bernie Quint
Technique: Colored Inks and Cello-Tak

(279)
Subject: Peace Works
Description: Poster
Client: Artists Against the War
Technique: Pen and Ink

(280)
Subject: The Birthday Party
Description: Film Promotion Symbol
Client: Palomar Pictures International
Technique: Pen and Ink

(281-284)
Subject: Computers Will Talk
Description: Advertising Brochure
Client: Madison and Wall
Art Directors: Frank Jansen / Les Gore
Technique: Pen, Ink, and Cello-Tak

(285, 286)
Subject: Lightnin' Hopkins!
Description: Album Cover (Front and Back)
Client: Poppy Records
Art Directors: Milton Glaser / Kevin Eggers
Technique: Pen, Ink, and Cello-Tak

(287, 289)
Subject: The Muggers
Description: Magazine Illustration
Client: New York Magazine
Art Director: Walter Bernard
Technique: Pen, Ink, and Wash

(288, 290)
Subject: Her First Taste
Description: Magazine Illustration
Client: New York Magazine
Art Director: Peter Palazzo
Technique: Pen, Ink, and Wash

(291, 292)
Subject: Grapefruit
Description: Magazine Illustration
and Sketch
Client: Look Magazine
Art Director: Phil Sykes
Technique: Pen, Ink, and Colored Wash

(293)
Reference For Plates 291, 292

(294)
Subject: Dangers of Radiation
Description: Book Illustration
Client: Andre Sauret
Art Director: Peter Knapp
Technique: Pen, Ink, Colored Wash,
and Cello-Tak

(295)
Subject: You Are What You Eat
Description: Film Poster (Unpublished)
Client: Peter Yarrow
Technique: Collage, Brush, and Ink

(296, 298-300)
Subject: Tempest
Description: Drawings (Unpublished)
Technique: Pen, Ink, and Wash

(297)
Reference For Plates 296, 298-300

(301, 302)
Subject: Nude in a Chair
Description: Poster and Sketch
Client: Paris Review
Technique: Silkscreen

(303)
Subject: Nudes
Description: Magazine Cover
Client: Push Pin Graphic
Art Directors: Milton Glaser / Seymour Chwast
Technique: Pen and Ink

(304-309)
Subject: Death In Venice
Description: Promotion Design and Sketch
Client: Warner Brothers
Technique: Pen, Ink, and Water Color